The True Identity

Jose Zapico

Our Vision

Reach the nations bringing the authenticity of the revelation of the Word of God, to increase the faith and knowledge of all those who fervently long for it, through books and audio and DVD materials.

Published by
JVH Publications
14900 SW 30th St. Unit 277566
Miramar, FL. 33027
All Rights Reserved

© 2025 JVH Publications (English edition translated from Spanish)
First Edition 2025
© 2025 Jose Zapico ©
All rights reserved.
ISBN 1-59900-168-3
© Jose Zapico. All rights reserved. No portion of this book may be reproduced, stored in a retrieval system, or transmitted in any form or by any means (electronic, mechanical, photocopy, recording, or any other) without the prior permission of the publishers. Except for brief quotation in printed reviews.

Cover and interior design: Esteban Zapico y Lidia Zapico
Translation to English by Hugo Lozano
Images and illustrations: Used with permission of Shutterstock.com.
Printed in USA
Category: Christian Life and Theology

Index

Prologue	1
Introduction	7
Chapter 1 *Identity Crisis in the Society*	11
Chapter 2 *The Consequence for Lack of Identity*	23
Chapter 3 *How to Recover Lost Identity*	37
Chapter 4 *The False Identity of the Church of Laodicea*	49
Chapter 5 *The Importance of Identity in Christ*	59
Chapter 6 *Discovering Your True Identity*	81

Chapter 7   93
Acknowledge it!

Chapter 8   111
Your Christian Identity

Chapter 9   125
Immorality Nullifies Authentic Identity

Chapter 10   137
How to Be Free from Sinful Habits

Chapter 11   145
Repentance as a Security Code

Chapter 12   157
Maintaining Moral Purity

Chapter 13   171
True Identity and Eternal Destiny

Bibliography   183

PROLOGUE

Knowing identity is one of the most valuable and important things for the human being. When you don't know who you are, you won't be able to know where you are going. As born-again Christians through faith in Jesus Christ, we have a new identity.

Knowing this, you will also know what is the purpose for which you were created, and you will understand the destiny that God prepared in advance for your life.

The enemy knows very well the importance of knowing who you are in Christ. This is the reason why he has always tried to distort identity, because in this way he disables human beings from fulfilling the purpose that God has for them. This is one of his ways of hindering God's work on Earth. To this end, it uses, among other things, lies, deceit and falsehood.

The person who is sure of his identity in Jesus Christ and who knows well the purpose and design of God for his life, will not be deceived by the subtleties and plots of darkness.

The first lost identity trait is: holiness.

The word "holy" means "separated, set apart, consecrated, pure." Our Father and Creator calls us to identify with Him, to have the same identity:

"You must be holy because I am holy." 1 Peter 1:16
When Adam and Eve sinned, they ceased to be holy, they no longer resembled God in likeness or image, they were separated from Him and lost their identity. They chose to disobey their own free will, exercised the right to act according to their free will and misused it.

Since then, everything has been messed up, and from that moment until today the whole of humanity has been searching everywhere, trying to find answers to the many questions that remained pending about its existence. Humanity is not clear about its destiny; this is the reason why there is an identity crisis in most people these times more than ever.

Ignorance of the Word of God produces an identity crisis with terrible consequences.

Judges 2:10 KJV
And also, all that generation were gathered unto their fathers: and there arose another generation after them, which knew not the LORD, nor yet the works which he had done for Israel.

Hosea 4:6 NKJV
My people are destroyed for lack of knowledge. Because you have rejected knowledge, I also will reject you from being priest for Me; because you

have forgotten the law of your God, I also will forget your children.

But learning and living according to the Word brings maturity and wonderful consequences. It is to recognize that today, there is a deep identity crisis among ministers, leaders, and believers in general. There is no reverence for the Word of God, most listeners do not care if what is preached or taught is true or false, just that it makes them feel good and motivated.

When the lack of identity leads you to live without making a biblical judgment about what is right and wrong, you only speak unsubstantiated opinions, and everything becomes a human philosophy.

By reading this book you will be able to understand that there are certain things that you must get rid of in order to live in your true identity. Remember that insecurity occurs because of not knowing the Word and therefore the real spiritual capacity is weakened.

On the other hand, there is the danger of diluting the message of the Bible, that is, altering the true gospel and the manifestation of the kingdom of God have their own identity, and when this is not done, the church is usurped of its identity, transforming it into a social Club. You cannot walk forward until you know who you really are in Christ Jesus.

Identity is something so important, so it must be understood that God created each one of us in a particular way. There may be millions of millions of people in the world, but no one is identical to another. The Creator, in his infinite wisdom, has made us different from others in certain things: fingerprints, the iris of the eye, voice and DNA.

Identity is a set of characteristics that are characteristic of a person and that allow them to be differentiated. But as children of God, we want to look like Him.

One of the devil's plans is to steal and alter the true identity of men and women, so that they cannot know who they are, so that they can never see themselves as reflecting the image of God.

Thousands of those who have accepted Jesus Christ as Lord and Savior of their lives are generally not capable of understanding all the blessings that have been bestowed upon them and continue to fail to recognize the new identity, they possess by having a new life in Christ.

Ephesians 2:12-13
That at that time you were without Christ, being aliens from the commonwealth of Israel and strangers from the covenants of promise, having no hope and without God in the world. But now in Christ Jesus you who once were far off have been brought near by the blood of Christ.

It is to understand that when you are born again you have eternal life, you are in the process of sanctification, you have a new way of living and you also have a new identity, you are already complete to be able to live the life of abundance that Christ gives you.

You will only become fulfilled and satisfied when you find your true identity in Christ. Yes, that is the very identity of the children of God: members of a holy nation, of a chosen people, heirs of the greatness of God, those who are called more than conquerors.

The Author.

INTRODUCTION

Why do we see more and more people who don't know what they want? Or that nothing in life satisfies them? Why is there so much violence and discrimination? Why are there more divorces and divided families every day?

The reasons are many, but the root of most of the problems in our society is the lack of identity. The triumphant life of a believer begins with a deep identity in Christ.

Our society suffers from a lack of identity, that is why the forces of evil move in the big entertainment and media industries to give people an identity that does not come from God.

The Word of God tell us: *"Love not the world, neither the things that are in the world. If any man love the world, the love of the Father is not in him. For all that is in the world, the lust of the flesh, and the lust of the eyes, and the pride of life, is not of the Father, but is of the world. And the world passeth away, and the lust thereof; but he that doeth the will of God abideth for ever.* **1 John 2:15-17** KJV

The world, through Babylon, offers an identity that goes against God, a materialistic and superficial identity. When people do not have identity in Christ, (they do not fully understand that they are children of God) it creates a void and a lack of identity that will then be replaced by the world.

The spirit of the world of this century is that of Babylon. You have to remember that when the people of Judah were exiled to Babylon, 70 years later they had the opportunity to return to the land of Judah, but most did not.

The reason was because they adapted to Babylon and once, they were accommodated to the system they decided not to return to Judah, even when they had the opportunity to do so. Not only that, but God spoke to them through the prophets that it was necessary for them to return and rebuild the cities of Judah, but many did not listen. The comfort and pleasures that Babylon offered were very difficult for God's people to reject. But God used a remnant that did return to Judah and rebuild the Temple and Jerusalem preparing the way for the coming of the Messiah into the world.

In these end times we find ourselves in a similar situation. The world has a lot to offer; and many, even the chosen ones, prefer the pleasures that it offers instead of doing the will of God in their lives. That is why John, in one of his epistles, reminded believers that everything the world offers, along with its desires and vanities, will pass away, and that only those who do the will of God will remain. It is important to put our priorities in order in these decisive times.

Our priority, as it was Jesus', is to do the will of the Father in our lives. May our longing and desire be to please God above all else. The identity that Babylon wants to give is material and temporary. But the inheritance of the children of God is eternal.

Galatians 3:29 NLT
And now that you belong to Christ, you are the true children of Abraham. You are his heirs, and God's promised to Abraham belongs to you.

Through Christ, we receive the promise given to Abraham, and we are heirs with Christ of all the blessings that come from the Father, which are eternal and do not compare with the vanities of this world.

The wise Christian understands that the greatest treasure is in eternal life with God. One of the first things that Babylon changed to the exiled Jews were their names. But although Daniel's name was changed to Belshazzar, he chose not to defile himself with Babylonian customs.

The name gives us identity and the identity that the heavenly Father gives us is more powerful than the one that this world wants to give us. The identity of Christ in our lives is the sign that will separate us from the things of this world and keep us focused on our calling.

God wants a generation willing to follow Him, as did the remnant of Judah, willing to rebuild fallen altars and destroyed walls. A people willing to reject the Babylonian system to do a great work before Jesus comes once more to earth to establish his kingdom.

Esteban Zapico
Youth Pastor
JVH International Ministry, INC.

CHAPTER 1

Identity Crisis in Society

One of the biggest problems that today's society is going through is the identity crisis. What human beings perceive as identity is very distant from what the Bible teaches. At this time, confusion and ignorance abounds around this issue.

When the enemy of souls manages to strip a man of his identity, he is in control of that person.

Someone who does not know who he is will be manipulated in his way of being, lifestyle, personal interrelationship, and his morality.

Mark 3:11-12 KJV
11 And unclean spirits, when they saw him, fell down before him, and cried, saying, Thou art the Son of God.

12 And he straitly charged them that they should not make him known.

There is a human identity, and there is a spiritual identity.

Regarding the text you just read, there is an important point to develop. The demons knew who Jesus was. Why? Because the Lord had an identity not only physical but spiritual. It is very important that you know who you are in God, but also to know in what position you are in the presence of the Lord.

What allows someone to recognize himself is what defines him as an individual, and a child of God.

You have awareness of identity, because you have memory, without it would be impossible to maintain a correct image of yourself.

Your identity cannot change because your genetics cannot be altered.

Some people say that the problem of sexual inclination towards people of the same sex is cause by a gene that has been altered. But scientifically it is known that there is still no human mind capable of understanding the human genome, and that can say that the human being has an alteration of a gene that inclines him to that state of immorality. That issue is medically ruled out. Today the identity of the human being can be influenced by the environment that surrounds him. For example, if all the people think that something is good, and it becomes fashionable, then that subtly generates in the person an acceptance towards that model that is being implemented, and they will begin to think that it is good.

In other words, the idea is being created that if a large majority agrees with an issue, and even the laws endorse what that group thinks, then the decision that was made is the correct one.

God the Father created the human being with a clearly perfect identity; however, how did the enemy manage to make man change the way he perceives himself? The enemy knows that if the person's way of thinking is changed, due to his evil influence, he will be able to upset his moral conduct in the midst of a society favorable to all degrading and perverted acts.

The Bible establishes in a clear way, that the times of this generation are the most dangerous that have existed on earth.

He even points out that there are nineteen types of personalities with a false identity that will be the common denominator in recent times, such as lovers of themselves, misers, stubborn men.

What does Francis S. Collins Think?

The American geneticist Francis S. Collins, who was one of the scientists who directed the human genome project, discovered in the perfection of genetics, the basis of powerful hands that created such wonder which led him to a full conviction recognizing Jesus Christ as Lord of his life.

He had to admit that man is not the result of chance, but of the divine designs of an Almighty God.

When man discovers the human genome, he has found the way to understand that the individual is the consequence of a divine science and not of a cosmic explosion. God uses science to affirm what He has already spoken by His Word. The human genome is what gives each person their identity and has to do with their genetic history; The immorality of the human being is not simply inherited but is the consequence of a state of curse that is transferred from generation to generation.

What Is Spiritual Identity?

The one that will make you strong to overcome everything you are facing. The evil spirits knew that Jesus was the son of God, and the Lord told the spirits "...don't tell anyone who I am". It is impressive to see that the demons knew the true identity of Jesus, while the scribes and Pharisees rejected him as the promised Messiah.

When the human being has problems in his spiritual identity, he will have conflicts with his physical identity; because he will not have the power to overcome the attacks on his mind, confusing himself and believing what is not. The spirits of immorality that surround this world oppress people who are weak in their personality, turning their physical and spiritual lives into captives, even though that has never been God's will for them. God's will is that none perish, but that all come to repentance (2 Peter 3:9).

The root of all human conflicts is the lack of spiritual identity. The worst thing that can happen to believers is not knowing their position and authority in Christ. Each one is a spiritual being living in a body of flesh and blood. When God breathes into the human being, he places in him a spirit of life; spirituality governs not only the interior but also the exterior. Jesus said, "out of the abundance of the heart, the mouth speaks." When what comes out of a person's mouth is pollution, dirt, and filth, this is a sign that spiritual life has been damaged and altered. What Christ wants to do in every believer is to also restore his spiritual identity.

If you believe in yourself less than others, you will always be hiding behind others. Obviously, what is going to be seen externally is the serious problem of what is inside you.

There is a huge difference in the genetics of a man and a woman. How is it possible that the human being gets to confuse that?

Remember what happened at the beginning when man wanted to group himself as a society that did not need God, we find that in the book of Genesis.

Genesis 11: 4 KJV

...And they said: Go to, let us build us a city and a tower, whose top may reach unto heaven; and let us make us a name, lest we be scattered abroad upon the face of the whole earth.

In the beginning, man wanted to build a city in the shape of a tower, a community to reach heaven, and be able to worship the god Baal. Nimrod's purpose was not to seek the presence of God, but to find a spiritual portal that would communicate with the solar deity they worshipped. With this I want to show you that not only the physical identity (the genetics of Adam and Eve was altered), but also the spiritual identity. There was no longer the need to worship the true God but the false god Baal, who represented confusion and deceit.

What is society achieving right now? Isn't it distorting their concept of morality to unite and worship false gods? What did they do in Detroit? Build an image of Satan and place two smiling children next to it; that is, this was a subliminal message that makes it clear that his intention is to change the mind of this generation, wanting to show that he is good and loves children. When it is Baal himself who wants to abort and destroy them before they are born, this is inconceivable!

God the eternal Father, promises the way to recover the distorted identity, through Jesus Christ his beloved son. It is not because of the world's religions, humanism, or philosophy; it is through Jesus Christ, who not only changes identity, but also brings us back to the Father's house, to communion with God; to the original position that we must have as children of God. There are still men and women who can testify that this is true!

When Paul was in Athens and saw the idols of the Greeks, he quoted one of his own poets as saying:

Acts 17: 26-30 NLT

...*26 "From one man he created all the nations throughout the whole earth. He decided beforehand when they should rise and fall, and he determined their boundaries.27 »His purpose was for the nations to seek after God and perhaps feel their way toward him and find him -though he is not far from any one of us. 28 For in him we live and move and exist. As some of your poets have said: "We are his offspring". 29 And since this is true, we shouldn't think of God as an idol designed by craftsmen from gold or silver or stone. 30 »God overlooked people's ignorance about these things in earlier times, but now he commands everyone everywhere to repent of their sins and turn to him".*

The Correct Identity

How does God give you legitimate identity?

Your true identity is called Jesus Christ. You cannot have Him and think as the world thinks, love what the world loves and hear what the world hears. There must be a marked difference between you and the world.

Ephesians 4:23-24 NKJV
..."*and be renewed in the spirit of your mind, 24 and that you put on the new man which was created according to God, in true righteousness and holiness*".

Romans 8:29 NKJV
"*For whom He foreknew, He also predestined to be conformed to the image of His Son, that He might be the firstborn among many brethren*".

What these biblical texts refer to is that human identity is restored the greater knowledge of God there is in a lifetime. If you are not regenerated from glory to glory and perfected in the image of Christ, you may run the risk of walking around as a spiritual wanderer with no identity. Romans 12:1 explains how every day you have to renew your mind to gradually adopt the identity of Christ.

God wants to return you to the Father's house.

He wants you to know what your true identity is, your heritage, your destiny. Everything that belongs to the Lord also belongs to you, including eternal life. A new life requires a new identity. The Lord is going to lead you to a new life transition and a restored identity with Christ because of the faith you have in Him. This does not mean that you will be changing from an old religion to a new one, what it means is that Christ is coming to dwell with you and give you a new life giving you the only true identity that communicates you with your Heavenly Father, who is the only Almighty God.

CHAPTER 2

The Consequence for Lack of Identity

Right now, the whole world is facing a loss of identity. Millions of inhabitants on earth do not know the purpose for which they were born and exist. There is a "false" identity that people think is okay to adopt, but it is based on wrong trends.

In the different media, more and more you can see the spread of this slogan: ..."it is not what you are, but what you want to be". However, let us analyze this true word:

Colossians 1:15-20 NLT
15 Christ is the visible image of the invisible God. He existed before anything was created and is supreme over all creation, 16 for through him God created everything in the heavenly realms and on earth. He made the things we can see and the things we can't see—such as thrones, kingdoms, rulers, and authorities in the unseen world. Everything was created through him and for him. 17 He existed before anything else, and he holds all creation together. 18 Christ is also the head of the church, which is his body. He is the beginning, supreme over all who rise from the dead. So he is first in everything. 19 For God in all his fullness was pleased to live in Christ, 20 and through him

God reconciled everything to himself. He made peace with everything in heaven and on earth by means of Christ's blood on the cross.

What Is True Identity?

According to the dictionary: it is the peculiar character or personality of each individual. Remember that each person has been created with God's purposes, and within that identity, He has established character and personality in each one.

When there is a false identity, there is a false character and therefore a false personality.

This is because sin has distorted the true identity that God has forged in each life. The consequences of having a false identity are the alteration of the true character and personality that each one should have according to God's divine purposes. The miracle of the new birth in each person who has recognized Jesus as their Lord and Savior, must bring a change in character (which is incorrect and deformed by sin) and therefore receive the correct identity according to the model of Christ and not of fallen nature.

Most humans have identity crisis. There is no defined identity.

It seems that the enemy of the soul takes

advantage of this deficiency and increases it. Nowadays, passports are being designed where the gender with which the person was born must be placed, but if for some reason they do not identify with that gender, they can be defined as neutral. That means that the person does not know that he is, neither one thing nor the other. The identity of the human being is going through a crisis, which is still a strategy of the infernal deception of the last days.

There are two types of identity:
1. Biological
2. Spiritual

The identity with which man is born is disrupted by the fallen nature and sin, and therefore affects behavior as the person develops. Sin not only changes behavior, character, personality, instincts, but also what he wants or wants in life. Precisely this disorder of what is lacking in accordance with God's plan and objective, is fostered most of the time from childhood.

The great question of humanity is why did I come into the world, and why was I born?

Humanity was created to have an identity; God did not create Adam and Eve in the Garden of Eden to leave them without a clear purpose. He did not say to them: "Make it up as you can, for this is your business." No, God established them with a plan, a design. He created them so that they would learn to trust what was prepared for them beforehand.

When there is no identity of what you are in God, it is difficult to be able to totally depend on Him. Many at this time are pressured by the demands of the world, because they listen more to the voices from outside than to the living Word of God. For many it is easier to walk where the crowds go than to know what God wants done. Few seek to do His will in their lives.

Humanity was created with an identity and the lack of that identity creates confusion.

The world is confused, young people and children do not know who they are, and a part of the Church is deceived because it has lost its identity in adoration, praise, prayer, or in the way people are reached for Jesus Christ.

No matter what happens, your identity cannot be altered by the plans that the enemy has against humanity.

In order for humans not to have a wrong concept of themselves, it is necessary to reach out to certain institutions such as the family and the community to tell them what the divine purpose was established for them.

The lack of identity is causing a tsunami that is trying to destroy families, which is the foundation of society. While the false identity leads you to be a slave to bad character, God wants you to understand that there is an identity that He wants to lead you to, so that you can be strong when others are weak. You are called to be an overcomer no matter what the world does.

A question that can be asked at this time is: what gives you the identity of belonging to a family? Surname. Each surname is identified with a particular family. Your name is a personal identification, and the last name is a hallmark that makes a difference. The lack of identity in a person can be generated by those who were abandoned, by those who were adopted, or by those who never knew their biological father or mother. Many families are on the verge of disappearing, due to a false mentality that has nothing to do with the will of God.

Many families created communities and live in certain regions in their countries.

Many determined to keep their lineage pure, as they did not marry people who lived outside their group or clan. Today there are many types of identity: cultural, national, racial or gender, all this is leading humanity to an intense crisis in relation to the correct identity. All this is a wrong way because it is not the concept that the Bible reveals. There are people with many prejudices because they are very confused. Human beings live in states of disorder, distorting divine concepts, principles and parameters and this condition directly prevents the purposes designed from eternity from ever manifesting. If Satan manages to confuse and place a false identity in the person, he will confuse him and make him feel rejected or with low self-esteem, since a lack of it will affect his emotions and even his physical health.

It is amazing that humanity is willing to die for these false identities and that they never know the real and true purpose of God in their lives.

Living a degraded life and far from God's will, will bring as a consequence: frustration, defeat, weakness. The false identity that you inherited generationally has nothing to do with the identity that Christ through his death and resurrection will give you, and instead of breathing death you will be able to breathe life; and instead of being defeated, you will be victorious.

In many communities there is a desire to disintegrate what is commonly known as the traditional family; When there is a divorce or separation, people often argue that there is a "character incompatibility", these are excuses that come up because there are battles that families do not know how to fight and that are the result of an identity crisis. It is important to know what your identity in Christ is so that you do not fall victim to irreversible attacks.

Identity in Numerology

During World War II, when Jewish prisoners were persecuted, they received a personal identification number, with a mark. They were stripped of their names, their nationality and even their beliefs. The identity crisis is a mental, psychological, humanistic confusion and it is a disorder that attacks at any age due to the conflicts, demands and pressures of the world. For the enemy, the human being is simply another number. That is why in the apocalyptic time they will be sealed with a mark. The number 666 is a perfect code that the enemy found. The number is a false identity that the world has. In many congregations, people are a number. There are many people who have lost their identity and do not know who they are; that is why they must be affirmed in the Word, and that they be built on the rock that is Christ so that when people convert, the concept of a lack of identity is changed by the correct identity that the Father gives to those forgiven and cleansed by the Blood of the Lamb.

Receiving and having a correct identity will keep you from being defeated in a spiritual confrontation. Many people get stuck in the past and all that it reminds them of. Many people cling to what they have stored in their home or in their thoughts. They always remember what they were and come to idolize a lifestyle. In Russia, Stalin, the first thing he did was take away the memories of the entire population. He stripped them of everything they had.

When people have a false identity, Satan steals everything from them, even the principle of honesty. If someone is arrested, they don't let him in with his clothes, but they take everything from him and put on a uniform. They are left without an identity to hold on to. Stripping a person of their identity is the fastest way to control, manipulate, and keep that life deceived.

Where is all this leading? Who can give a genuine and true spiritual identity?

Lack of identity enslaves people and robs them of blessings. People addicted to surgeries and to changing their physique because they don't feel good about themselves, they don't care how many surgeries are done, their problem is still spiritual. God created Adam and Eve with an identity. When Jesus was born in Bethlehem, in Luke 3 we are given his genealogy. He was born with a purpose; the Father had sent him, and he came from an offspring that Satan wanted to destroy; the genealogical line by which the Savior of the world would be born according to the prophecies. When Adam and Eve were deceived, from that moment on, not only their identity, but that of the entire human race, was distorted. In the Garden of Eden, the first thing that was stolen was the identity. It is evident that they were dressed in a heavenly garment like that of the angels and when they lost their identity, they saw themselves naked. When they were determined to listen to the serpent, they went into rebellion, at the same time they were stripped of everything.

How does God the Father solve the problem of the lost clothing of human identity?

Adam and Eve tried to dress in fig leaves. But still in the sight of God they were naked. The only thing that the Father would accept is the model that He himself designed; God made a sacrifice, the first one spoken of in the Bible, the first sacrifice God made to cover the man and the woman. He dressed them in animal skins. He covered them because they had failed and were about to be thrown out of the garden. It was a way to protect them because if he didn't, Satan would take more fury on them.

Man throughout the history of humanity has tried to cover himself in the wrong way. He has done it through his religions, his idolatry and paganism, his wrong practices, and still the man is still naked, trying to simply cover himself with some leaves; but what God did in the garden of Eden was a prophetic figure of what he would do in the future on the Cross of Calvary. Only God could cover man and woman, and although the sacrifices and the shedding of blood did not take away their sin, he did cover them in a certain way.

God wants to take away the sin that overwhelms you and that you stop being naked, and that you cover yourself with the garment that the Father forged on the cross through the sacrifice of Christ.

When you receive Jesus in your heart, He puts on you the garment of grace because each one of your sins has been forgiven. The devil will no longer be able to do what he used to do, because he sees you dressed in garments of grace. If for any reason you try to remove the garment of grace you are wearing, Satan will tear you into rags, and he will completely destroy you. What covers you is what gives you the correct spiritual identity and makes you understand that Satan cannot destroy you because you are dressed, and he cannot attack and harm those who are correctly covered but only those who are naked to make them his slaves.

If at some point, you lost your investiture of grace, recover it at this time because for you, the consequence of a false identity will be terrible. If you keep dressed in grace, when He takes you, he will make a move and take away your grace dress, for a bridal garment, fine linen, white and resplendent because you will already be prepared for eternity.

There are times in life when Satan brings conflict, oppression, and many fall into defeat and failure, inevitably losing the original garment with which God clothed them. There are times when Satan tries to put pressure on you, bringing conflicts and imbalances into your life. It is there when the enemy can attack and weaken you; but the Lord wants to free you and walk not as a slave, but as a free person by the Power of Jesus Christ. Come to the Lord; ask him to dress you in the garments from which you were stripped by sin, and to put the garments of grace back on you, so that you may be invested with the identity of Christ.

Have you weakened in your spiritual life, and you wonder why?

...it is perhaps, because you try to do things your way... if you know that God is Almighty to do things better than you, why try to change with your human strength, when in reality it is impossible. Possibly you are hiding behind a tree like Adam, or your own justification and you say: "after all, I am not as bad as that one..." here the issue is to say to God: "forgive me, I was wrong, I have a mistaken concept of me, I think that I do not need anything or anyone, when in truth, I need you with all my heart.

When you try to do things your way, you take off the garments you are dressed in, and that is the exact moment that Satan is waiting for. That you strip yourself of the true of God, to dress yourself in a false identity.

I invite you to pray this Prayer:

"Father, thank you because I am not just another number, I am not the result of a coincidence, I am the result of a divine design, formed and created by your own hands, I am not what the world thinks, nor what the devil wants me to be." You call me by my personal name and only you through the perfect sacrifice of my Lord and Savior Jesus Christ have given me the true Identity."

CHAPTER 3

How to Recover

Identity

In the United States it is very common to give each generation a specific name. Did you know that in this country there are six correlative generations that have been defined? Let's break this down for a moment:

1.-The generation, **"GI"** between 1901-1926.
2.-The **"mature"** generation is between 1927-1945.
3.-The generation, **"baby boomers"** between 1946-1964 (or the postwar generation).
4.-The generation, **"X"** between 1965 to 1980.
5.-The generation, **"Y"** or the **"Millenium"**, between 1981- 2000.
6.-The sixth generation, **"Z"** or the **"light booms"** from 2001 onwards.

This latest generation has marked the difference between the previous five generations. In each one of them there have been transformations, but in this last one is where the most changes have taken place, it is the generation that has lost "its identity", they are confused about who they are and where they are going.

In the history of humanity there has not been a generation like the one we are mentioning. There is a lack of correct definition of true identity, and about themselves. The economic and family instability and the excessive fantasy that access to the technological revolution has brought, has upset the true purpose of life and has created an abyss of separation between the spiritual and the fantasy; reason why "the self" has taken control in the heart making it believe that it does not need the Creator.

From the beginning of creation there was an attack against the identity of the human being.

In the Garden of Eden, Satan managed to elaborate a subtle strategy to steal the original identity of the human being. There, both the man and the woman lost the image and likeness of God as a consequence of sin and this produced an alteration in their genetics and in everything that the Almighty had created perfect in them.

Undoubtedly the plan of darkness against humanity was carried out; the identity was completely distorted, while the human being contracted death and degradation within himself.

Today, the attack on identity continues.

It is very evident that in this generation of the 21st century, it has been highlighted by technological and scientific advances; however, it cannot be denied and ignored, which has been where there has been more degradation, moral deviation, and lack of ethics in all areas. It is like going back in time, when humanity was continually inclined to evil, as described by the Word of God in the book of Genesis.

When I speak of identity, I am not only referring to fingerprints, but to the specific characteristics of each person themselves. God has assigned to each one a purpose and a unique plan in a particular way. What God has designed to do with a person is something unique and individual; the Lord works with each one in an extraordinary way.

God's gift is a renewed mind, a new heart, a healthy body.

All this strengthened by the grace of the Holy Spirit. When you discover who you are in Christ and that you have received authority to be victorious over all evil works, you will be able to go against the enemy with the power of the Name of Jesus.

Remember that Jesus came in a human body but without ever knowing or practicing sin.

I invite you to observe the conditions in which He was born.

-His birth was not favorable, and his family was not wealthy (He was born in a manger).

-The political situation at that time was very hard, because his country was ruled under the opprobrium of the Roman Empire.

-He grew up in Nazareth, where the Bible says that nothing good would come of it (John 1:46).

-When the angel told Mary that what was in his womb was from the Holy Spirit, the family and religious leaders murmured, doubting his virtue.

Despite these unfavorable conditions, the identity of the being that was gestating in the womb of Mary was not affected or lost its value. Jesus always knew who he was, and why he had come into the world. He was fully aware of what his purpose was when coming to earth, he knew the will and plan designed by God his Father, which would be fulfilled in his life to give salvation to humanity.

You cannot lose your identity because of the conditions in which you were born, or because of what you are facing right now. If you know the reason why Christ saved you, you will live a life of total victory and not constant defeat.

It is important that you fully discern the priority reason why Christ forgave you, without failing to understand that he gave you his saving grace, even when you were weak, and your thoughts were not aligned with the mind of God. Today you must know who you are in Christ! By placing your trust in Him, He will give you full certainty of recovering what Adam, as the first man, lost.

The moment you recover your identity, you will no longer be what the enemy wants you to be a slave to sin and dominated by works of evil, because you will have the identity of Christ, and you will know that you can do everything because He strengthens you.

The first thing the Holy Spirit wants you to understand is that God does not want you to imitate others to feel better. Be always yourself! You can be influenced in the faith and faithfulness of others, but in the Lord, you must have your own identity based on who you are in Christ. Always ask for what He has prepared for you, walk in the activation of his promises.

Remember this example: What was the role model of the Apostle Paul? Did he not say: ..be imitators of me, as I of Christ? He went to the same Lord, whom he loved and served.

The Uncertainty of Today

When I talk to people, I constantly ask them:
What plans do you have?
What are God's dreams in you?

The True Identity

Most of them don't know what to answer me, especially when I ask them who they are in God, because they don't know what to do in the near future. They need guidance, it's like a society without goals, very fickle. Think about this: if you are in Christ, you will receive identity and you will be free from instability. The Bible says that: "If the son of man sets you free, you will be completely free." He who has full identity in Jesus will be free of frustrations and lack of identity. If you don't know what God's destiny is for you, you will live wrong models.

Many young people seek to imitate rich and famous people in the world, this happens because there are not enough "role models", people of integrity in their leadership who bring a genuine image of the Savior to follow and imitate. When you have an identity recovered through Christ, God will provide you with the genuine pastor or apostle who will guide you to imitate the only role model that is Christ. He is an eternal friend, who will never leave you, you must follow him in love, fidelity, and loyalty to Him and to His Word. Your recovered identity model should be called only Jesus Christ because He will never fail you.

Colossians 1:15 NTV

"Christ is the visible image of the invisible God. He existed before anything was created and is supreme over all creation.

What is Recover in Jesus Christ?

The lost family is recovered. The lack of identity is causing a tsunami that is trying to destroy families, which is the foundation of society. While the false identity leads you to be a slave to bad character, God wants you to understand that there is an identity that He wants to lead you to, so that you can be strong when others are weak.

You are called to be an overcomer no matter what the world does. Many families are on the verge of disappearing, due to a false mentality that has nothing to do with the will of God.

In many communities there is a desire to disintegrate what is commonly known as the traditional family; When there is a divorce or separation, many times people argue that there is an incompatibility of characters, however, they are excuses that come up because there are battles that families do not know how to fight and that are the result of an identity crisis.

Many people are searching for a lost identity. In Jesus Christ there is hope so that every man and woman can recover their genuine and true identity. The image and likeness with which God created you. You are part of a chosen people and more than conqueror in Christ Jesus.

Romans 5:19 NTV

"Because one person disobeyed God, many became sinners. But because one other person obeyed God, many will be made righteous".

The Bible says that no matter how hard you try to be faithful and obedient to God, if you continue to have a false identity it will be impossible to achieve it. The fallen nature had adopted a condition of sin that from then on would be inclined to disobedience. When he chooses for himself, he chooses badly; the human being always tends to make mistakes when he chooses. Adam transmitted sin to his children and these to all men. Sin was already in the genes. Genetics were altered and that is why the Blood of Christ, which is Holy and perfect, needs to cleanse you of all contamination.

Genesis 3:3-5 NTV

³ It's only the fruit from the tree in the middle of the garden that we are not allowed to eat. God said, "You must not eat it or even touch it; if you do, you will die". ⁴ "You won't die!" the serpent replied to the woman. ⁵ "God knows that your eyes will be opened as soon as you eat it, and you will be like God, knowing both good and evil."

When Satan seduces them, they are deceived and manage to distort the identity with which they had been created by God to live eternally and not to die. They had the correct genetics, the perfect

DNA, but everything was altered as a consequence of their disobedience before their Presence.

This teaches you that when man disobeys God everything is altered and confused. The devil's purpose is to get you to lose the design and plan for which you were created.

Psalm 51:5 NTV
"For I was born a sinner, yes, from the moment my mother conceived me".

Sin degenerated all aspects of man's life. When God sees you in sin, separated, far from Him, in your own walk; he looks at you with an identity that is not yours but the one the enemy gave you; but that is why Christ, the Son of God, appears to give you the correct identity and undo all the plans of iniquity over your life. What the inexhaustible and perfect love of an Almighty God has done is that our identity is restored. Jesus was willing to pay the price to restore all things, so that the devil no longer sees you with a false identity, but with the correct identity; with a new authority that strengthens your inner being.

The identity of marriage is in God who formed it and blessed them to be one. Each one must take his role to form those parts that come together. This wonderful plan of God has not ended, Christ came to reaffirm it when he died for his beloved

Church. While the enemy came to kill and destroy, each one is responsible for maintaining heavenly harmony in each home.

CHAPTER 4

The False Identity of the Church of Laodicea

One of the things that unfortunately is happening in these times is that the Lord's faithful are confronting the false Church, the one that claims to believe in Jesus Christ but has lost its identity.

Revelation 3: 16-18 NLT

16 But since you are like lukewarm water, neither hot nor cold, I will spit you out of my mouth! 17 You say, "I am rich. I have everything I want. I don't need a thing!". And you don't realize that you are wretched and miserable and poor and blind and naked. 18 So I advise you to buy gold from me — gold that has been purified by fire. Then you will be rich. Also buy white garments from me so you will not be shamed by your nakedness, and ointment for your eyes so you will be able to see.

In these biblical texts it is Jesus Christ himself who speaks, and he refers to a Church that those who professed the faith were lukewarm. They all lived indifferently; one thing was the same to him as the other. That opens the door to tolerance. The believer becomes tasteless and useless.

Like salt that no longer does its job and is useless. God is of no use to such a Christian, that's why he removes him from the body. That is why at this moment there are so many people going from congregation to congregation, trying to hear something that is pleasing to their ears, avoiding hearing what God really wants to speak to them. When people only want to feel comfortable somewhere, it is to silence their own conscience; unfortunately, they will never develop spiritually, until they die of spiritual malnutrition.

You don't need to be a Word theologian to understand we have reached an era in which the Church is as lukewarm as Laodicea.

One of the things to understand is that this generation is spiritually lukewarm. The loss of identity produces spiritual blindness and deafness. People no longer set their sights on Christ and his Word but on whatever instantaneous thing that nothing else satisfies their personal needs. However, Jesus speaks saying:

Revelation 3:19-21 NLT

...[19] "I correct and discipline everyone I love. So be diligent and turn from your indifference [20] » Look! I stand at the door and knock. If you hear my voice and open the door, I will come in, and we will share a meal together as friends. [21] Those who are victorious will sit with me on my throne, just as I was victorious and sat with my Father on his throne.

Jesus warns that whoever has ears, hear what God is speaking to his Church through the Holy Spirit. The gospel is not a religious practice, but rather a lifestyle; we must follow the instructions of the Word which makes us fit to present ourselves before God.

People who are in apostasy justify themselves by stating that the thousands of people who fill their temples bear witness that all is well. I want to tell you something, the fact that there are crowds in a Church does not certify that what is done there is correct.

The lie of the churches with a style like the church of "Laodicea", is to make people believe that they live a life pleasing to God, when the truth is the opposite. They do not realize that the Lord Jesus Christ will return at any moment and those who have not borne fruit will not go with Him. The most alarming thing is that there are people who have grown on the solid foundation of the gospel and are now sharing and accepting that false identity based on a way of being "church" that is not true, because it says that the Lord will vomit it out of his mouth. God is not moved by the crowds, because many hide behind the masses, pretending a spirituality that they do not have. The lukewarm Church represented in Laodicea will never be able to have power and authority to confront darkness. This style of Church that has a false identity is destined to be thrown out of the body of Christ.

Jesus said that because she is blind, she cannot be the vehicle of Christ on earth.

She becomes a source of anger and loathing. The true Church of Christ is triumphant, despised by the world, persecuted by others, but it is protected because it remains faithful to Almighty God. This Church differs from the others, because it knows what it is to live walking next to God, and it knows purity and holiness. He also knows how to walk in the revelation of light and not in the shadows of darkness.

They enjoy a spiritual discernment, because the more they seek God, the difference between light and darkness can be seen.

The true Church does not boast of what it has, but is invisible, and longs expectantly for the Lord to come soon. The Church that anxiously awaits the return of the Lord groans before the Presence of God, so that He returns because of the evil on earth; there are too many abuses towards children, and society in general is increasingly degraded and perverted. The true Church cannot mix with the behavior of the world, because the only one that wants to please is God, according to the commandments of his Word. Unfortunately, in this day and age many are more concerned with what the world thinks of them, and with pleasing others than with obeying what the Holy Spirit says.

When you stop fearing God, and the Word no longer has any effect on your life, you are in grave danger, you are entering the degree of lukewarmness. The Bible says:

John 15:18-19 NLT
18 If the world hates you, remember that it hated me first. 19 The world would love you as one of its own if you belonged to it, but you are no longer part of the world. I chose you to come out of the world, so it hates you.

Luke 21:12 NLT
"But before all this occurs, there will be a time of great persecution. You will be dragged into synagogues and prisons, and you will stand trial before kings and governors because you are my followers."

The Persecution Continues

For many centuries, men and women of God have been burned at the stake, and sacrificed as we now see in the Middle East. In China, thirty temples were recently destroyed, and in some places in Mexico, such as Chiapas, evangelical Christian churches are burned. In Nigeria, Somalia and other parts of the world, deaths and destruction of churches continue. The Bible says, "all who want to live godly in Christ Jesus will suffer persecution." But the most important thing to note is that it also says, "Those who love their life will lose it, but those who hate it will win it because of me." The world says: "love your life, protect your life, seek to be protected, no matter what others go through". The Church without identity approves and accepts leaders who are in tune with the world. A pious man will somehow suffer trials, persecution, slander. Jesus said: "Woe to you, when all men speak well of you, for that is what their fathers did with the false prophets."

If a Christian agrees to act according to the example of the Church in Laodicea, it can only be the result of having denied the cross and the blood that Jesus shed on it. The Laodicean Church lost compassion; the Spirit of Christ was not in them. Today it is the same, there is no compassion for other people's pain, humanity has gotten used to it.

The true church is the one that prays, cries out, and identifies with the pain of others; she is the one who wants to see souls free from abuse, violence, and abandonment.

The Church of Laodicea says: I have everything, I lack nothing, I am on all the TV channels, in some countries you can say: "I have all the millions of dollars that anyone would like to have...", but they do not have the power to ease human pain. What good is it for them to have so much money, if they do not have the Spirit of compassion in them? At this time the true Church not only confronts the evil thoughts of the world, or the immoral laws that are approved in the nations at a global level, but apart from that, the so-called Christianity that lives in apostasy. A Church that claims to be, and is not, that claims to have and does not have; that claims to know the Word and does not know it, because with its actions it denies it.

That Church that acts like the Laodicea has in itself a mixture of concepts that are not approved by God.

The Church of Laodicea did not worry about the soon return of the Lord; mix the music of the Spirit with music dedicated to demons, the same thing happens today, these churches say that Jesus will not return until they dominate the world. Jesus said that an evil servant is one who says in his heart, The Lord is slow to come. This type of teaching has arisen due to the spiritual decay of thousands of spiritually lukewarm people, who refuse to go after the cross. When love for Jesus is kindled in hearts, there is a longing for his soon return. When we are filled with the Spirit and seek the Presence of God, there is a continual desire to be with Him and behold His glory as close as possible. The opposite of Churches with false identities is when sin abounds, while they repudiate the denial of the same self. This haughty way of walking brings increased growth, because there is no demand for the true gospel of Christ.

1 Corinthians 15:51 NKJV
Behold, I tell you a mystery: We shall not all sleep, but we shall all be changed!

Who will be transformed? Those with a true identity, or those with a false identity?

The true Church of the Lord worships Christ above all things, and He is the center of everything. The Lord can never be replaced by anyone, much less by a denomination. He must be the most important thing in your life and family.

CHAPTER 5

The Importance of Identity in Christ

When it comes to recovering the lost identity from a human perspective, previously it was totally impossible, all human beings were lost in their own condition of sin.

Paul in his letter to the Galatians makes the difference between before and after Christ.

Why is it important to have an identity in Christ? What is the importance of knowing who you are in Him?

If you truly come to know your identity, you will have a very valuable possession in your life. When the human being does not know who he is in Christ he cannot know where he is going, nor what is the purpose, design, or plan of God in his life. When this happens, you live a weakened, failed, frustrated, and defeated life. But by being born to a new life through the power of redemption and regeneration, God changes your identity, and you go from being removed from his presence to reconciled with the Lord and brought back to the original state for which He created you.

In Christ you will know not only what was the purpose for which you were created, but also what

is the destiny that God prepared in advance for your life.

The true identity of the human being has been distorted and by not knowing the plans that God has assigned for life, he becomes incapable of fulfilling the purposes for which he was called.

There is an appetizing terrain for the enemy of your destiny, and it is your mind; if he manages to place thoughts of frustration, defeat and weakness you will be ready to fail completely. That is why it is important to know that there are characteristics of God's character that He wants to impart to your life, with the purpose of modeling you in his image and likeness, such as the following:

Mercy

God is merciful and it pleases Him to impart to His children that way of being, and it is to be full of mercy to help those who need it. In the Sermon on the Mount Jesus said: "Blessed are the merciful, for they shall obtain mercy."

Love

God is love, and he delights in pouring out his perfect love on us so that we can give it to others.

This is part of the process of forming God's character in us. Similar to Jesus himself, so that you may grow to the stature of the perfect man. Every day, God presents you with a new challenge, goal and design that He himself established in you.

God has extraordinary purposes for your life; but Satan somehow has the ability to hinder the work of God in you and for this he uses harmful strategies so that you never discover what your identity is and live totally oblivious to that authority that is power, victory and strength.

Jesus was inside a human body, however, when faced with trials or temptations, He remained without doubt always knowing that He was the Son of God. Within himself he was not unaware of the reason why the Father had sent him to this world, and what was God's plan designed and established in him.

Jesus was never confused about who he was and what he had to do.

In the most difficult moments, he never lost the correct orientation of what to answer and how to act. There are people who say that he is powerless in the face of his weaknesses, affirming that God understands him and accepts him as he is. However, the Bible says: "... say the weak I am strong."

Jesus defeated the attack of the enemy without showing his great power, he did not need to do it, the true anointing never shines. Jesus did not have to prove who He was.

You don't have to prove who you are in the Lord. Never fight in your own strength.

At the right time, the Lord is going to reveal who you are in front of everyone, even in front of your own adversary.

When Jesus was tempted in the desert by Satan, his enemy's main motive was to make him doubt, in some way, his true identity as the Son of God.

There are many people who have lost sight of their identity in Christ. Jesus did not have to prove to anyone about who He was, because he knew very well that he was the anointed one, destined for a mission within the divine plan of his beloved Eternal Father. This example gives you strength for when you have to face the battles in your own mind. When the enemy tells you: "if you are so spiritual, do this or that...", it is because you are spiritual. Satan always knew that Jesus was the Son of God. That is why he said to him: "... if you are the Son of God."

The first thing that Satan will attack is your identity that characterizes you for your calling and places you within God's plans for your life.

You must strongly believe that you are not what Satan wants you to be, but what God called you to be. Do not believe the lies of the enemy so as not to live in defeat and confusion. God has created you and has allowed you to live in this world so that you can recover your identity and be used by Him for His glory and honor. When you have full conviction of who you are because he gave it to you, you will be a new person in your decisions, in your thoughts and in your way of living.

Matthew 4:2-3 NLT
² "For forty days and forty nights he fasted and became very hungry. ³ During that time the devil came and said to him: —If you are the Son of God, tell these stones to become loaves of bread".

When Jesus came to earth in a humanized form, to fulfill the redemption process by saving man from sin, the enemy wanted to confuse Jesus so that He would not fulfill the purpose for which He had come. From the time Jesus is born until he reaches the cross, he is continuously stalked and has a constant battle against the power of darkness.

The enemy tried to keep Jesus from reaching the cross. He told him: "...make these stones become bread, if you truly are the Son of God..." he practically told him: ... "if you are the Son of God you have the power and authority to turn these stones into bread". Satan is not going to ask you a question if he is not convinced that what you have is the truth. If the enemy had not known that Jesus was the Son of God, he would not have tempted him the way he did. What did Jesus use to defeat him? The spoken Word. Jesus said: "...The Lord your God you shall worship, and Him alone you shall serve."

What was the enemy's plan to tempt Jesus in the desert?

If he managed to get Jesus to disobey God, this would impede the purpose for which He came to earth and therefore lose His identity as the only begotten of the Father.

What worries the enemy is the design, the purpose and the plan that God has for your life.

Remember that you have your own fingerprints, your unique genetics in the iris of your eyes, the record of your own voice. He reveals to you in a tangible and real way that you are unique, there is no other like you. God makes originals and not clones.

The enemy knows that if you are not sure of your identity, you will fail quickly, and this failure will be the cause of the postponement and impediment of your being able to experience a true life in Christ within your being.

What is the challenge of discovering the purpose for which you were born?

Design is to develop and grow. Upon you there is an inheritance of eternity; For God to grant you that inheritance, you must be mature and have the correct spiritual stature, so that you know how to minister what God puts in your hands.

In the Hebrew custom, it is very normal for the son to receive his inheritance at the age of thirty. He has to wait and reach that age, so that he is given what he deserves for being an heir son. It is for this reason that Jesus received the inheritance from him at the age of thirty, that is; He began his ministry here on earth at that age and not before. That is why the Bible says that when the believer grows and develops, he has the capacity to be heir to everything.

What is the first trait of identity that was lost in Eden, and that through Christ was recovered?

The first missing trait according to the Bible is holiness.

1 John 4: 16 NLT
We know how much God loves us, and we have put our trust in his love. God is love, and all who live in love live in God, and God lives in them.

Psalms 111:9 NLT

He has paid a full ransom for his people. He has guaranteed his covenant with them forever. What a holy, awe-inspiring name he has!

What does the word "holy" mean? Set apart, separated, consecrated for a purpose. It also says that we have been conceived in sin, and that because of our sins we have been deprived of the Glory of God. But the Bible also says that God put in Christ the sin of all humanity, that is, of all people. Jesus said, "Father, sanctify them in Your Word."

Our creator calls us to identify with Him and have the identity with which He has formed us. If God is Holy, He calls us to be holy as He is holy. That identity of being holy can be transferred to us. A holy person has life and has been sanctified by the blood of Christ.

When Adam lost his endowment and was cut off from God's presence, who did he look like now? To God? No! He was more like the one who held him captive for sin. Because the enemy was disobedient to God, he made sure that man was also disobedient, that he sinned and thus lost his identity. It is from that moment that man enters into a crisis of his identity with God.

But in Christ we can recover it even if we have lost it at some point in life.

Identity is so important that God created humanity in a very special way. Your identity as a child of God, redeemed and forgiven by the Blood of Christ, your desire must be to become more and more like Jesus. The enemy came to kill, steal and destroy lives, purposes and plans designed by God, preventing God's promises from being activated. Therefore, the human being who has lost the correct identity is prone to falling into weakness, frustration, and defeat.

On earth today there are more than 7,200 million of people, and no one is identical to another. God has made each person different and have their own characteristics. The enemy's strategy is that you do not know who you are in Christ, so that you do not see the reflection of the image of God reflected in your life. When one does not have the identity of Christ, it is because the person does not believe himself worthy of receiving God's forgiveness. When you can't recognize who you are, this is a clear and obvious sign that you have no identity.

For example, there are many who declare the following: "I am useless, I will never achieve what others achieve, I was only born to suffer." There are many people within the churches who are not sure if they are going to go to heaven, or if they are worthy of the blessings of Almighty God. Many live this way in a state of uncertainty. There are people who think that what God did with them is over and they have no more plans.

Get ready because God is not done with you. In the Bible it says that God is building your life.

That means that if He is building your life, it is because God's construction is still in progress. He is going to use a stable foundation, the same rock that is Christ, to establish you. He will lift you up on the hope of glory, and he will give you promises from God, which will lift your faith and give you a destiny of glory.

What Concept Do You Have of Yourself?

If you think you are the same as everyone else, you are wrong, you are different! If you think that the same thing that happens to others is going to happen to you, you are wrong, what God promised you is going to happen to you. Believe in the divine promises and appropriate them!

When you have accepted Jesus Christ as your Lord and Savior, your new believer mentality has not absorbed everything necessary with your new life, it has not developed, nor have you fully assumed the identity of Christ, this is a gradual process.

> **You have to renew your mind every day in the Lord.**

You can't keep thinking according to the old mentality you had. You have to allow the power of the Word to establish the correct thoughts and completely uproot all contrary thoughts, which lead you to ignorance and frustration, instead allow the Holy Spirit to align your mind in the purpose to which you were called, to the full design of the identity you have in Christ.

Ephesians 2:13 NLT
But now you have been united with Christ Jesus. Once you were far away from God, but now you have been brought near to him through the blood of Christ.

According to what the biblical teaching determines, before we were children of disobedience and children of wrath, separated from the Father, but in Christ we have been reconciled with God, forgiven, and justified before the Father. And God does not see us as something strange but as children, having been freed from the mark of guilt that the enemy had placed in our lives as a result of sin and disobedience. In Christ we have eternal life, and we are in the process of sanctification, we have a new way of living, an identity in Christ, we are already complete to be able to live the life of abundance that He gives to each one of those who are willing to surrender before Your presence. Assume it in your mind and accept it in your heart!

Romans 12:2 NLT

Don't copy the behavior and customs of this world, but let God transform you into a new person by changing the way you think. Then you will learn to know God's will for you, which is good and pleasing and perfect.

You have a new life, a revived spirit, a strengthened body, but if you do not have a renewed mind, it is of no use to you, because the mind is part of your integral being. God, in the Bible, left us examples of people who did not know who they were and how he had chosen them. They did not know his identity.

Let us remember the examples of Gideon, Saul and the prodigal son.

These three people lost their identity or rather are identified as those who did not know who they were in God. However, Gideon recovered his identity through the intervention of the angel, while Saul did not value the position in which God had placed him and lost it by disobeying him. Therefore, it is important that you reflect and ask yourself: What is recovered when God establishes identity? Lost spiritual clothing, authority and footwear.

When your identity in God is restored (after it has been distorted, damaged, and stolen by Satan), Jesus Christ will give you a new spiritual garment and completely exchange that fallen nature for a glorious life in Christ. Authority will be returned to you through Him, who was constituted "the last Adam", to walk the correct path that will lead you to triumph, and the glorious plan established and promised by God for your life.

1st Case: Gedeon

Judges 6:12 NKJV
"And the Angel of the Lord appeared to him, and said to him, "The Lord is with you, you mighty man of valor."

When the angel of the Lord appeared to you, what did you call him? Strong and brave young man. Gideon did not understand why he called him that, if he was scared, hiding the few bunches of wheat that he had left, because the Midianites would come and steal all their food. What was that an act of bravery or cowardice? He was hiding it and kept it inside a cave, and in the midst of this situation the angel of the Lord found him.

Gideon had a destiny and design; therefore, the Lord has to challenge him to break the pattern of his mind.

And when he does, God declares what Gideon is..." a strong and valiant man". When he speaks to her through the angel, he is assuring the identity that he has. On earth Gideon is trembling, but in heaven there is a record that says, Gideon, brave and strong. The devil made him believe that he was nobody, but what God had established was written in heaven.

When Satan says something to you on earth, it is not the same as what God has said about you. Many say like Gideon: "I can't, it's difficult, others can, I can't...others can, I can't".

When the enemy comes to attack you with all his subtle instruments of deceit and lies, get ready because he is going to tell you what you are not. But God will have to change the erroneous scheme of your mind, letting you know what He designed in his divine plans for you.

The angel told him, not only strong and brave but... "I am with you, go and save Israel... I do not command you." Gideon continued to show his insecurity when facing the Amalekites, and yet he manages to gather thirty thousand men. How many did he keep? Not even with ten percent, only with one percent, if only with three hundred men. What defines the brave are the attitudes of how they conduct themselves before God and have a heart full of courage. The brave is capable of doing what no one does, while others are trembling, they speak what no one speaks and do what no one dares.

2do Case: Saul

1 Samuel 9:20-21 NKJV

^{20} But as for your donkeys that were lost three days ago, do not be anxious about them, for they have been found. And on whom is all the desire of Israel? Is it not in you and on all your father's house? ^{21} And Saul answered and said: I not a Benjamite, of the smallest tribes of Israel, and my family the least of all the families of the tribe of Benjamin? Why then do you speak like this to me?"

Saul is in an identity process. His self-esteem is completely destroyed, he has a completely negative self-concept. He was the tallest, handsomest, and strongest young man in all of Israel; However, when the prophet announces to him that he will be the first king of Israel, he does not consider himself fit for that position, he does not dare to do what God says, and even when God changes his heart, he was afraid that the position of The king was too big for him and he hid. He didn't feel capable.

1 Samuel 10:22 NKJV

Therefore, they inquired of the Lord further, "Has the man come here yet?". And the Lord answered, "There he is, hidden among the equipment."

When God chooses you for something, you have to be sure that He is not wrong and will never stop fulfilling His Word.

When God points you to something, don't say: "Lord, I don't know how to do it, I can't, I don't have the capacity." When you recover your identity in the Lord, nothing is impossible for God.

3rd Case: The Prodigal Son

Luke 15:13-17 NKJV

13 "And not many days after, the younger son gathered all together, journeyed to a far country; and there wasted his possessions with prodigal living. 14 But when he had spent all, there arose a severe famine in that land, and he began to be in want. 15 Then he went and joined himself to a citizen of that country, and he sent him into his fields to feed swine. 16 And he would gladly have filled his stomach with the pods that the swine ate, and no one gave him anything. 17 But when he came to himself, he said, "How many of my father's hired servants have bread enough and to spare, and I perish with hunger!

The prodigal son came to his senses when he realized that he was a son and went to regain his identity. The pressure has been so strong and suddenly you have become weak, and your heart no longer longs for anything that God has for you, and you settle for the carob beans that are thrown to the pigs. The prodigal son came to his senses, and realized who he was... he thought that in his father's house, the day laborers lived better than him. The prodigal son got up and went again to his father's house to ask for forgiveness. Your identity is restored when you recognize that you have failed, and you repent. That is the key for God to restore you. To the prodigal son everything was restored, and he recovered everything.

In the story of the prodigal son, we see that the father made the son recover everything.

The Lord clothes you with grace, changed your garment of defeat for one of victory and completely restores your true identity as an heir son. The Father places a ring on his hands. He regained the authority he had lost. He also put a shoe on his feet, to claim his territory. You will no longer be barefoot, but you will step on snakes and scorpions (figures of evil spirits), because now you will have the appropriate footwear on your spiritual feet, to step on all works of evil with authority, with security and conviction that nothing can harm you.

We see in these three examples, with one who had lost his identity completely, another who was in a state of rejection and low self-esteem, and the last one who had lost everything.

The Eternal Father justifies you through the shed blood of Jesus.

When someone turns to God saying: "I have failed, I have made a mistake, I have disobeyed you, I have lived according to my will, in a disorderly way, please forgive me, I am sorry." The Lord will change tragedy into inner peace; your abandonment, for the great family of God, giving you the garment of authority which no one can take away from you.

Which of the Three Do You Identify with Today?

It may be that you have lost your identity in Christ and not realized it. It may be that you have stopped recognizing that you are hardworking and brave. It may be that God wants to take you out of the cave of fear, fear, insecurity and you try to get others to do what God told you to do and Satan tells you: "that is not for you", that is his strategy to keep you in the cave where no one sees you.

The Lord tells you that what is written in heaven is different. God has a written record of you in The Book of Life. Everything you do and what you are going to do is already written in heaven. In Revelation he says that on the last day, God the Father will give the order and the book of life will be opened, in which everything is recorded. What

God has written in heaven for you will be executed even if the devil tries to prevent it.

Ask God to give you a correct identity in Him as his child, as the one He has called to serve Him and love Him forever.

CHAPTER 6

Discovering Your True Identity

We must know that "if something false exists, it is because what is true has previously existed." The false is a projection of something that there is something that is true. The Bible talks about how to know what is false and what is true. How to discern darkness from light and the difference between obeying and not obeying God.

When you know who you are in God, you know your purpose and you know why you exist on earth. When you don't have identity in Christ, you don't know what your calling is in your life.

Lack of identity cause insecurity and distrust.

That was one of the most crucial battles that Jesus faced against Satan himself.

Luke 4:1 NLT
Then Jesus, full of the Holy Spirit, returned from the Jordan River. He was led by the Spirit in the wilderness,

In this biblical passage what led Jesus to the desert was neither his emotions nor his feelings, but the Holy Spirit of God. When you have the true identity of God, everything you do, you will do according to the will of the Spirit and not of your flesh. The same Spirit will direct you and you will know what to do. I ask you a question: Did the Spirit of God know in advance what Jesus was going to confront? Of course, he knew it, for Him there is nothing hidden or occult.

If the Spirit of God knew that Jesus would face a bitter and subtle enemy, for what other reason would Jesus have been taken to the desert, besides praying, and seeking the face of the Father? Jesus knew his identity, but the devil had hatched a strategic plan that is revealed in what is described in the book of Luke.

Luke 4:3 NLT
Then the devil said to him, "If you are the Son of God, tell this stone to become a loaf of bread."

When you are not sure of the identity of Christ, you do things out of emotion and feeling and to demonstrate to others how high the spiritual degree, power, or authority you have received is. Jesus did not need to make a public demonstration to the devil of who He was.

Jesus knew perfectly well that He was the Only Begotten Son of God. Did the devil know that Jesus was the Son of God? He did, so why does he insinuate to him... "if you are what you think you are, show me?".

The first spiritual battle that is fought when someone is going through a desert is a war against one's identity, this battle seeks to create a doubt in your mind. If the enemy manages to open a breach, he will always have the opportunity to attack through that gap.

The toughest battle that every man or woman who has surrendered to Jesus is facing in this hour, regardless of age, color, race, economic position or knowledge, is the battle of their identity in God.

It was in that area that Satan first confronted the Lord. But Jesus said to him: "I don't have to make any demonstration to you of who I am." Jesus told him something like: "My Father did not send Me to give demonstrations to you, because I know that My identity is that I am the Son of God, the Father has sent Me with a plan why and for what and not to give you exhibitions. , but to destroy you, because you are that serpent from Eden and you are going to know that I am going to step on your head, defeating you.

You have to know the reason why God has forgiven, saved and cleansed you. He has not called you to bring out your gifts as something that is something of yours that you can show to your admirers. The first thing you are going to demonstrate to the devil when you have a true identity is that the truth that is within you is to glorify the Name of the Lord. Not even your ministry, rather, the call of God in you. Satan will be completely disarmed. And he will say: "I am facing someone who knows who he is."

The worst thing in this hour of deception and apostasy is that there are thousands of believers who do not know who they are in God, for that reason the enemy can do what he wants with those people, and always have them in spiritual defeat.

Every time they want to conquer new goals they fall into problems; they never achieve something concrete. They escape a hole and fall into twenty. It is a repetitive cycle of failures, frustrations and defeats. But if you close every fissure or crack in your mind, you are free in your heart from doubt and unbelief and you seek God that will determine not only your victory, but it will also define your eternity.

Whatever comes, difficulty or struggle, you can never forget your purpose in God.

You always have to believe and trust in God. True identity is not emotional or sentimental. It is based on the truth of God and his Word. He is real, no matter what comes upon your life or the attacks the devil throws at your life; Your true identity should not be based on circumstances, but on the Glory of God, the magnificence and power of Him. No matter the conditions that surround you, you are still a child of God.

You should not listen to just any message; take care of your ears.

There are messages that a Christian child of God should not hear. You cannot hear a preacher approving of your disordered state of sin; On the contrary, you must listen to the one who challenges you to be better than you are today. You need to hear a message of power that helps you develop your identity with God. You don't need a motivator, but a true word from God that leads you to change your lifestyle. Paul said:

Colossians 2:8 NLT
"Don't let anyone capture you with empty philosophies and high-sounding nonsense that come from human thinking and from the spiritual Powers of this world, rather than from Christ."

What is your identity based on? In theories, false arguments, or in the traditions of impious men? The opposite is to rely on Christ alone. Paul once said: "These people are not supported by Christ", we must make sure that a person's teaching is totally established in Christ, because when a biblical passage is misapplied, it can easily become a weapon in the hands of the enemy.

If you do not know the entire concept of the Word of God and apply it incorrectly, you can fall into error.

The enemy believed that simply by declaring "it is written" he could easily defeat Jesus. It is true that the enemy knows more about the Word of God than many Christians, with the difference that he uses it to manipulate and control according to his convenience. The devil suggested that Jesus jump from the top of the pinnacle of the Temple, naming him the word that is written in Psalm 91, ...he will command his angels near you.... If Jesus had not known the Word well, he would not have been able to defeat him, however this word was misguided and Jesus knew it, that is why he was victorious.

Unfortunately, many Christians today do not read the Bible, much less scrutinize it, so when someone appears, distorting the Word, they easily fall into error.

You have to know the Word more than the devil knows it. Jesus knew which text he was quoting, but since He knew the Word, He told him: "I'm going to tell you something, My Father is going to protect me, I don't have to tempt Him by jumping off the fifth floor. My Father tells me that he will send the angels around Me to guard me in all my ways so that my foot does not stumble against a stone."

There is a huge number of people who believe everything they are told, for that reason they are easily deceived, because they do not like to study the Word. You cannot hear messages that cover up people's sin, the Word of God will never exalt evil more than the work of Christ.

True identity aims to please God.

A true child of God whose identity is forged in Christ will not exalt sin, because he knows that in the Kingdom of God, the norm is to please the one who called him from darkness to his admirable light.

He who pleases God is pained by the serious consequence that sin leaves.

Colossians 1:12-14 NLT

12 "giving thanks to the Father who has qualified us to be partakers of the inheritance of the saints in the light; 13 He has delivered us from the power of darkness and conveyed us into the kingdom of the Son of His love, 14 in whom we have redemption through His blood, the forgiveness of sins".

The focus of being a true Christian is not to stop sinning simply to achieve an identity. Stopping from sin must be a result of the work of the Holy Spirit done in your life, for who you already are in Christ. People think... "I'll stop doing this, because God will give me this"; For this reason, many find it difficult to understand it, and they use God as an amulet, not as a model to follow, which is why many do not like to be told about holiness and purity.

Galatians 3:3 NTV

...How foolish can you be? After starting your Christian lives in the Spirit, why are you now trying to become perfect by your own human effort?

Paul said... "It cannot be that they begin in the Spirit and end in the flesh." The normal thing is to begin in the flesh and end in the Spirit. This happens when you defocus from Christ to only see your mistakes, failures and weaknesses; This will remain in you only until you change your attitude and begin to focus on Christ; taking away the old way of living.

The power of death and life, of the Cross and the Blood of Christ, made you fit to have a true identity.

It would be a big lie to tell you to fight against sin with your own strength, you have to put to death in you the works of the flesh that fight against your salvation. Stop focusing on yourself! When you focus on what you have, you will never need God, but keep in mind that this fallen nature that you feed, sooner or later if you do not make it die, will destroy you. Do you feel weak, fail, with mistakes? Come to God in prayer, look for the only one capable of removing the bad that is in you, this is called Jesus Christ and his Blood shed on the Cross.

Change yourself first and then others.

Sometimes the wife wants the husband to change or vice versa, getting into a fight or conflict and they say to each other: "if you change, I will change..." The issue is not what you see in others but what is in you. Sometimes the problem is with you. When you focus on looking at others and not what you have, you have no identity in God.

When you begin to look at Christ, and focus on Him, you will understand that He can free you from darkness, with His powerful hands.

The Lord takes you away from the kingdom of darkness and now you are in the kingdom of light, but you continue with bad habits, and you say: "Lord, I know that you forgive me for my sins...", and the Lord tells you: "let to look down and begin to look up." Sometimes you feel afraid like the hunchback woman in the Bible, you can't see Jesus, you only think about what you have and what you can't do, while God tells you: "Lift your face, something is going to happen!" "... when you lift your face and are able to look at the face of Jesus, you will be impacted by Him, you will be able to look into His eyes and you will desire His holiness while He will draw you to His purity and nothing will deceive you; From there, everything will change.

If people are not impacted by the same Presence of God, they will never be able to change. When you have an encounter with Him, you will be a new person. Stop fighting God because you can't escape what you can't change.

CHAPTER 7

Recognize It!

In the previous chapters, it has been mentioned about Jesus' experience in the desert and how He faced Satan and all his lies.

Mathew 4:8-10 NKJV

...*⁸ Again, the devil took Him up on an exceedingly high mountain and showed Him all the kingdoms of the world and their glory. ⁹ And he said to Him, "All these things I will give You if You will fall down and worship me." ¹⁰ Then Jesus said to him, "Away with you, Satan! For it is written, 'You shall worship the Lord your God, and Him only you shall serve.*

In this third temptation the Lord was faced with a very different one from that which He was confronted with in the first and second. The main objective of the kingdom of darkness was to rob Jesus of his true identity as the son of God.
At this moment humanity is confronted with the same war that Jesus fought in the desert. The enemy has launched a subtle attack to confuse the human being so that he does not know who he is, and what his God-given purpose in life is. He does not perceive under any circumstances, ''Who he is in Christ'' and what has been the extraordinary work that God carried out for each man and

woman through Redemption.

Remember that the Lord has transferred you from the power of darkness to the kingdom of his beloved son; The Word says that I uproot you from one place, to take you to another place, changing your position and condition through regeneration.

You will maintain your true identity in Christ, when you are completely willing to remain within his true will in the kingdom of God. Your identity was purchased and acquired by the perfect sacrifice of Christ.

As a human being you are limited, and many times you cannot see beyond the natural senses. Sometimes it seems like there is a battle going on between the natural senses and what God says through His Word.

The human sense that is most attacked by the enemy is sight.

In the temptations that Satan makes to Jesus in the desert, it can be seen that each time the test becomes stronger. On this occasion he tempted him by offering him all the kingdoms of the earth, in exchange for him changing the meaning of worship.

What does identity have to do with worship? In this passage it is demonstrated that the devil offered Jesus all the kingdoms of the earth, in exchange for receiving worship.

There are two things you should be clear about on this topic:

1. Your identity in Christ is not defined by your natural senses, nor by your emotional state.
2. True worship of God will give you a true identity.

It is interesting to observe how the devil has always wanted to obstruct the purpose of the children of God, in exchange for offering sin as worship. Jesus was about to begin the powerful ministry that the Father had entrusted to him. A ministry of power that was about to become public. In this you are seeing the fight that Satan wants to establish against the son of God through false visions and promises; That is why I reiterate that your identity will never be defined by your natural senses. The devil and the world have wanted to steal your identity as a child of God, that is the enemy's purpose. It is evident to remind you that identity is connected with adoration, it requires your time, finally it will become your passion and your particular dedication. Everything you value, and are willing to sacrifice, will become the object of your adoration. Your whole being can often surrender to the things you admire, and it is not necessarily the worship of God.

In this the senses play a strategic and important place because through them you can deviate from the true worship of God.

Adam and Eve were tempted in the same way, their senses and emotions were altered by Satan's lie; beyond the truth that God had spoken to Adam.

The senses defeat the purpose of true worship because they are connected to emotions.

The senses play an important role in worship, as many times, they will try to distort your approach to identity.

If there is a weakness in your fallen humanity, it is that the enemy will try to distort what you are seeing, to show you an "apparent reality" (which is not true) in order to steal your identity. How many times do you allow your thoughts and senses to deceive you in your characteristic as a child of God? Many times, you believe that your thoughts are correct and you find yourself battling feelings of guilt, religious lies, tricks of the devil to lead you astray; and you don't realize that they are darts of fire that battle against your mind.

There are many strategies that are being implemented at this time against you to try to steal and damage your identity.

How many times have God's children decided to believe in lies without realizing that they are gradually deviating from the truth? Perhaps now at this moment you remember a person who praised God like you and is now separated from the ways of God and you can help him find his identity as a child of God. What you have to do is identify what is true and what is a lie, you will never recognize this unless you learn to understand the big difference that exists between one and the other. When you believe that lies are truths, you will never live up to the level of a genuine and true identity.

Worshiping God is an act of faith You must worship God not because you see Him but because He is real.

You won't be able to see Him with your eyes physically, but you will know He is there. There is a truth that man or woman has not understood, and that is that true worshipers will worship God in spirit and truth. For you to connect with God you must have a defined identity, because Christ is absolute truth.

When you worship God, his Spirit connects with your spirit, and that will give you an identity of belonging.

What is worship and praise? When you communicate with God you must discern how you

do it and why you do it. When you begin to worship him, do not think about what surrounds you, because you make use of your natural senses, do not worry about who worships or who does not.
When you worship you are communicating with God and that is where He begins to minister deep in your spirit. Everything Jesus taught had a purpose. He said that true worshipers will worship Him in spirit and in truth. That means that there would be worshipers who would do it in lie or in appearance.

Worship is pleasing God, that moves his Spirit to respond to worship.

What Do People Think About You?

Today the lives of many Christians can be seen through a very powerful lens such as deception. One of those ways of deception is to always worry about what people think. The enemy places these thoughts in you so that you are very concerned about what others think, instead of what God thinks of you. Your identity is defined in God and by the things you worship. If you value an object, person, or whatever you have in your hands, and for you that is more important than Him, you become a worshipper of what you have. Anything that takes away the place that belongs to Him becomes an idol. The enemy knows what you like, and through that, he will try to establish a spiritual spell, trying to manipulate and control you. There are people bewitched by a subtle force of deception, in such a way that people are confused and many of these deceptions are religious lies or dressed in false humility.

Galatians 3:1 NKJV
...*O foolish Galatians! Who has bewitched you that you should not obey the truth, before whose eyes Jesus Christ was clearly portrayed among you as crucified?*

In the NLT Bible version, it says "O foolish Galatians, who has bewitched you...?" When people become followers of men, even though they are wrong, they are manipulated. The meaning of Jesus' death on the cross was explained very well to the Galatians.

When can you quickly identify your identity? How can you rebuke an enchantment if you do not know that it is manifesting? Charm is a spell, or a diabolical influence.

Jesus said to the devil: "Go away from me Satan" ...this is the way you should respond. When the lie comes, the erroneous thought must be identified, and do like Jesus, thought, deception, spell, leave me in the Name of Jesus, because it is written; and name the biblical text.

You will never have authority if you do not have revelation of the Word; you cannot be an effective worshipper if you do not know it and do not know how to use it with power.

You will not even be able to be an anointed musician, if you do not have revelation of the Word. Musicians and those who worship are the ones who most need to have revelation of the Word. The explanation is that the Word of God connects to your spirit; The Word reveals to you the principle that you have authority to rebuke and confront the spiritual world.

John 1:12 NLT
... *"but to all who believed him and accepted him, he gave the right to become children of God".*

Today we have worship in spirit and in truth, which is a means to receive from God, what He offers us, which is, his gift of life.

John 4:10 NLT
...If you only knew the gift God has for you and who you are speaking to, you would ask me, and I would give you living water."

Through worship, you enter heaven where the throne of God is, through the blood of Christ. There you feel the presence of God like never before and the Father who sits on the throne gives you the true identity of a son.

The identity of the Father is above personal emotions.

Emotions work opposing salvation. Always living under the design of your own state of mind is contrary to living by the Spirit of God. There is nowhere in the Bible that shows that God can be known by them. On the contrary, the soul and mind are described as enemies of faith because they always lead the person to doubt.

On the contrary, to receive life in the Spirit you must have a contrite and humiliated heart.

Psalms 51:17 NLT
The sacrifice you desire is a broken spirit; you will not reject a broken and repentant heart, O God.

Human experiences play a very important role in life, but they do not replace the Presence of God.

Many times, some get carried away by emotions and say things that are not based on the true revelation of the Word of God. No one can get carried away by emotions, they are often uncertain and dangerous. The Bible says: "There are paths that seem right to a man, but their end is the path of death."

Feelings come from the heart and sometimes they are not one hundred percent reliable.

Jeremiah 17:9 NKJV

...The heart is deceitful above all things, and desperately wicked; Who can know it?"

What God teaches you is that your emotions must be controlled through his Spirit. The believer under the direction of the Holy Spirit submits to Him to do the will of God acceptable and perfect. Often feelings based on emotions can make you feel like doing something in one way or another, and as you walk along that path, suddenly the Holy Spirit reminds you: "that is not the place, go back and return to the place." where you came from" while inside you there is a battle that does not want to accept the voice of God and you think: "forgive me, but I feel that I must go the other way", the Spirit of God is going to warn you again, but If you persist in doing what your thoughts tell you, denying what the Spirit directs you, then you will be walking towards a temptation that can lead you to the place of failure or frustration.

Exodus 13:21 says: that their God Jehovah went before them to guide them day and night.

We also read in Jeremiah 10:23 KJV "I know, O Jehovah, that man is not lord of his way, nor is it for a man who walks to order his steps."

The Word of God tells us that you are not the owner of your way, Jesus is the way to the Father. Emotions are not the way to the Father; the revelation of knowing the Lord comes when you have intimacy with Him.

How can you worship and connect with the Spirit of God to understand that you are truly a worshiper after the Father's heart? The answer is easy, if you have a relationship with Him, it is because you know Him.

If you are given the opportunity to participate in something in the Lord's work, do you first pray to prepare? Did you ask God what His will was for what you had to do? Can you hear God's voice clearly? Are you used to hearing his voice and knowing who God is?

The word "know" in Greek is /ginosko/ and means: "a frequent relationship between the person who knows and the person known."

To know God is to have a deep knowledge and relationship with Him.

That relationship leads you to intimate communion, which is achieved in worship done in the spirit. The more intimacy and the more relationship, the more knowledge. The less relationship and intimacy, the more coldness grows in your heart. Many people believe they know God, yet they do not walk in His ways.

How can you walk where He wants, if you don't

know Him yet?

> **To know Him is to want to please Him in everything.**

Many times, when I am studying the Word, I am shocked to the depths of my being, when I verify that this biblical text that I have read so many times, I am understanding in a much deeper way than before. Making rhema inside me. What is written, this happens when you invest time, and you are willing to sacrifice the hours that entertain you, to surrender them and give them to God, remember that He tells you to redeem the time because the days are bad.

There is nothing more excellent when at the moment of praise in a service, the Spirit of God descends on all those who worship, and a prophetic anointing of new songs begins to flow. It is not the time to wage war perhaps, but to continue singing prophetically, because every worship leader has to learn to flow in the river of God. The more you worship him, the more his glory fills you, and you are in tune with heaven, connected to receive from God what strengthens you.

> **The heavenly Father in worship connects with your spirit and only He can give you the identity of a Son.**

That is why worship is so important, it is the way to know who you are. When you know that it is not the opinion of others about you, that it is not your natural senses, but what God impregnates in you: an experience with his presence, that will make you confident.

It is not your righteousness; it is the righteousness that the Father obtained in his son for you. Because the justice that man can offer before the Father is considered rags, something useless or without applicable justification.

In the Word it has an even lower meaning, when it refers to the justice of man himself, it is: "like filthy rags". Something that is not valid, lacking value to be accepted as the "debt" to the guarantor.

The Father needed someone to pay the debt that sin left when it entered the heart of man, and only the blood of Jesus was the price of that costly debt, much more than gold bars or silver coins.

For this reason, adoration is the personal gratitude of one who understands that through the offering of Christ, our debt was paid to the Father. There is true gratitude in praise, it is when we worship Him, honoring the Son and the Father, for accepting the offering that Christ gave in our place.

How can we not have gratitude and praise when Jesus paid our debt?

Worship is "the fruit of lips that recognize the truth of divine justice." It is not simply a thought, or a song, it is a grateful heart that believes and understands the wonderful work of Jesus.

It is under the promise of God, given to your life that tells you: "I will always sustain you, with the right hand of my Justice."

That is why the true worshiper does so with the only and genuine truth that is born from the justice of the Father. Not that which exalts itself, but the true worship that is accepted by the Father, which is based on this absolute truth. Glory will always be to Jesus Christ!

Proverbs 3:5-6 NKJV
...*⁵ Trust in the Lord with all your heart and lean not on your own understanding; ⁶ In all your ways acknowledge Him, and He shall direct your paths.*

There is a very important word here and it is recognize it.

You Will never get to know God if you don't first recognize Him.

To recognize is to distinguish, identify a person among several people in a place. It is also knowing the characteristics of that person. The word recognition is to distinguish, so the application to this is easy: God will not recognize a person who has not known Him first. When I have a true identity, I am connected to the Father who gives me that identity, and because I recognize Him as the giver of salvation. The word recognition is also: examine carefully. Being able to examine a person to better understand their status and condition. To do this you must worry about understanding the truth of divine justice. Strive to investigate to delve deeper into divine revelation.

Then you will reach the following conclusion: How can you worship God without knowing Him?

Worship is born in the secret of prayer, in the intimacy of God first, because it is the consequence of the passion for him. In this continuous search, God himself reveals himself to your heart. When you recognize God as Lord, you hand everything over to Him. That act is "surrender," recognizing that He is a sovereign God. While you surrender, He gives you the security you need.

Psalms 9:10 NKJV
...And those who know Your name will put their trust in You.

When you accept that the Lord must be in

everything you do and are, you learn to depend on Him totally. You receive that revelation from Son, which leads you to wisdom, and teaches you not to rely on your own opinion. The more intimacy you have with Him, the more worshipful you are, the fewer mistakes you will make in life.

Proverbs 28:26 NKJV
...He who trusts in his own heart is a fool, but whoever walks wisely will be delivered.

If you understood every Word that the Lord gives you, and put it into practice, you would avoid many problems. Everything has its time, and everything has its purpose. I invite you to pray the following prayer before the Almighty God:

"Father, help me understand that I can only have my true identity when I worship you and recognize you in all my ways, because you straighten my steps. Help me to know more intimately every day who you are, in all the majesty of your glory and power, with all my being I thank you in this hour, for loving me the way you do every moment, help me make you faithful every day of my days , to surrender completely before your holy presence, and may I never lose the true identity that you have given me, for eternal life, it is in the name above all names of my beloved savior and Lord Jesus Christ that I ask all of this now and always, amen.

CHAPTER 8

Your Christian Identity

How many of you know who they are? They know your first name, last name and address.; Now, how many know their identity as Christians? In other words, what are they, what do they have and what can they do in Christ? I ask you right now: if you died right now, where would you spend the rest of eternity? In heaven or hell?

If your answer is: I don't know, and you have already received Christ in your heart, then you have an identity problem.

And if your answer is: I don't know, and you have not yet accepted Jesus as your Lord and savior, then you are right to worry about where you will spend eternity.

I. The Value of Identity

Your identity is a very valuable thing, if you don't know who you are, then you won't know where you are going.

As a born-again Christian by faith in Jesus Christ, you have a new identity, a purpose, a destiny; But the enemy has taken it upon himself to distort that identity with his lies and false beliefs, thus nullifying all effectiveness and power in your life.

It is evident that Satan continues to attack that area of the believer's life because he knows that the further away you are from your identity, the closer you will be to failure.

II. Meanings of Identity

1.- Identity.- identical quality. Identical means: "Same", "the same"

2.-The second meaning of identity is a legal meaning. Identity, in this sense, is the fact of being a person or thing the same as what is assumed or sought.

III. What is Your Identity Without Christ?

a) True identity does not come from what I am or what I have achieved, but from what God has done in me. (Philippians 3:4-9)
b) The world gives me a specific identity and is based on:
1. Who are my parents?
2. What nationality do I have?
3. What profession or job do I do?

c) The Bible declares that we were without Christ: (Ephesians 2:1-3)
1. Children of disobedience.
2. Children of wrath.
3. We did the will of the flesh.

We must be sure of our identity in Christ Jesus.

Ephesians 2:13 NKJV
But now in Christ Jesus you who once were far off have been brought near by the blood of Christ.

One of the things that human beings struggle with the most is identity, and this, in each of us, has to do with three questions that we must answer. Whoever knows how to answer them knows perfectly well what his identity is.

Who I am?

Think about it carefully because people are very confused when it comes to answering, not many manage to answer it or they do it wrong, but if you know how to answer it then you are well oriented regarding your identity. Knowing who you are is essential to knowing what your identity is.

Where do I come from?

This has to do with origin, with your past. If you

know where you come from, then you have a well-defined identity.

Where I go?

And it refers to the future, it has to do with your destiny. Do you know your destiny? Do you know well where you are going? Whoever answers these three questions is perfectly situated in life, knows why he exists, knows why he came into the world and what he has to do.

Virtual Identity vs. Real Identity

John 8:14 NKJV
Jesus answered and said to them, "Even if I bear witness of Myself, My witness is true, for I know where I came from and where I am going; but you do not know where I come from and where I am going.

Jesus was a person aware of where he came from and where he was going.

Matthew 16:17 NKJV
Jesus answered and said to him: Blessed are you, Simon Bar-Jonah, for flesh and blood has not revealed this to you, but My Father who is in heaven.

This biblical passage shows that Jesus knew who

he was, why?

Because while he was having a conversation with his disciples, he asked them who people said he was, then the disciples answered him that some people said it was Jeremiah, others that it was John the Baptist, others thought it was Elijah. And the Lord asks them:

And you, who do you say I am? Simon Peter answered and said: You are the Christ, the Son of the living God. Matthew 16:16.

Then Jesus said to him: Blessed are you Peter because this knowledge was not given to you from the opinion of people but is the revelation of my Father who is in heaven.

Jesus knew well that He was the Son of the living God just as Peter said. If you ask Jesus who he is, He will answer you: I am the Christ, the son of the living God. I know well who I am.

Who knows who they are, knows why they have come into the world, what they have to do and what their goal in life is.

It is important that you know your identity.

But there is an identity that has to do with what you think you are, with what your parents or people think you are, and this could really be called a kind of virtual identity.

What you think about yourself can limit the possibilities of what you should or can do. Many times, you can have a virtual identity, that is, a wrong idea of what you really are and when this happens you are limited in terms of knowing why you exist and what the true purpose of God is in your life and what you must do to achieve it.

There are many who believe that they will never achieve anything, for example, if your mother told you all your life that you are useless, that you are of no use, you have taken that identity as a virtual reality and you say: I am a /a useless and I will never amount to anything.

So, you work only to exist, but you do not have the ability to understand what the reason for your existence is, because you think about yourself that you will never amount to anything, and you will never achieve anything.

Do you realize how important the term identity is?

This virtual identity is affected by what you think or what people have thought about you.

Does my identity have to do with what I think I am or what people think I am?

True identity is nothing like that.

Remember that everyone had a different opinion as to who Jesus was, however, was Jesus Elijah or Jeremiah? No, it wasn't any of them! He had an identity that was not given by what people thought.

The Lord answered him: Blessed are you Peter, because flesh and blood has not revealed this to you, it is not the opinion of people, this has been revealed to you by my Father who is in heaven.

Therefore, Jesus is not what people think, He is what the Father reveals to Peter, and he already knew this before he received that revelation.

Identity Linked to Origin

A person is not what they think they are, but what God determined that person to be. Therefore, knowing who I am, has nothing to do with researching what I can do, what my father or people think I am, but rather I have to look for my true identity in God, because He was the one who created me and me. form.

The identity of each of us has to do with a genuine revelation of God into our lives. When a human being comes into the world, he is not born by chance or by mistake, God brings people into the world. He gives identity to people.

The issue of identity has become a serious

problem; Therefore, when people are born, they are registered immediately; All countries have a registry because it is important to identify them and for them to have their identity.

The true origin of identity comes through Jesus Christ.

Therefore, there is a virtual origin or a real origin. Many believe that we come from monkey or matter. When the Bible says that Christ gave His life for us and rescued us by shedding His precious blood on the cross of Calvary, He gave us life. When people have an encounter with Christ, they encounter his true origin, his true identity.

God said to the prophet Jeremiah: Before I formed you in the womb I knew you, and before you were born, I sanctified you, I made you a prophet to the nations. Jeremiah 1:5.

Notice the opinion that the people had of Jesus: Philip found Nathanael and said to him: We have found him of whom Moses wrote in the law, as well as the prophets: Jesus, the son of Joseph, of Nazareth. Nathanael said to him: Can any good come out of Nazareth? Felipe said to him: Come and see. John 1:45-46.

The people's idea was that nothing good could come out of Nazareth. Jesus grew up in Nazareth, the Messiah, the Deliverer, the Son of the living

God, not what people think. He is the lamb that was slain from the beginning. Christ was already the lamb sacrificed on the cross of Calvary when there was still neither world nor Calvary.

The Bible says I come from God! It also points out that God has thought of all things from the beginning and has known us before we were born, just as he knew Jeremiah and just as the Bible says that Jesus is the Lamb slain from the beginning of the world.

People are very confused; they don't know what their identity is. Men don't know if they are men and women don't know if they are women. Many say I have a problem; I am a man, but I feel like I am a woman. What an identity problem.

You have come into the world with some things more and others less. Now that is a drama. It came out wrong from the factory. There are many factories today that take responsibility if a product goes wrong and they fix it, or replace it with new parts, but God's factory is perfect. He knows who you are, what your origin is and what your destiny is, because God has given origin and destiny to everything he has made, and in his divine sovereignty there are no errors or failures.

Your identity is not something you have to search for. Many say that one has to go searching for it in life, but it is not that you can choose it among many identities but rather that there is only one identity for you, and it is God, and it is a revelation that he has to give you, to fully understand the identity. that He Himself has given you.

I invite you so that you can read and meditate on the great truth of the Word of God, which affirms your true identity as a Christian, through the following biblical texts:

- Psalm 139:1 "Jehovah, you have examined me and known me." **I am known by God.**

- Psalm 139:13 "You created my insides; You formed me in my mother's womb." **I am created and formed by God.**

☐ Psalm 139:14 "I praise you because I am an admirable creation! Your works are wonderful, and I know this very well." **I am an admirable creature.**

Psalm 139:16 "You saw me before I was born. Every day of my life was recorded in your book. Every moment was laid out before a single day had passed." **I am an object of His will.**

Romans 5:1 "Therefore, since we have been made right in God's sight by faith, we have peace with God because of what Jesus Christ our Lord has done for us." **I am justified.**

Romans 5:8 "But God showed his great love for us by sending Christ to die for us while we were still sinners." **Even though I was a sinner, Christ demonstrated his love and died for my sins.**

Romans 6:6 "We know that our old sinful selves were crucified with Christ so that sin might lose its power in our lives. We are no longer slaves to sin." **I am delivered from the power of sin.**

Romans 8:1 "So now there is no condemnation for those who belong to Christ Jesus." **I am forgiven and not condemned for my sin.**

Romans 8:15 "So you have not received a spirit that makes you fearful slaves. Instead, you received God's Spirit when he adopted you as his own children. Now we call him, Abba, Father." **I am a son of God.**

Romans 8:38-39 "And I am convinced that nothing can ever separate us from God's love. Neither death nor life, neither angels nor demons, neither our fears for today nor our worries about tomorrow —not even the powers of hell can separate us from God's love. No power in the sky above or in the earth below—indeed, nothing in all creation will ever be able to separate us from the love of God that is revealed in Christ Jesus our Lord." **I am secure in the love of God.**

Ephesians 1:3 "All praise to God, the Father of our

Lord Jesus Christ, who has blessed us with every spiritual blessing in the heavenly realms because we are united with Christ." **I am blessed spiritually.**

Ephesians 1:11 "Furthermore, because we are united with Christ, we have received an inheritance from God, for he chose us in advance, and he makes everything work out according to his plan." **I am an heir of God according to His will.**

Ephesians 2:10 "For we are God's masterpiece. He has created us anew in Christ Jesus, so we can do the good things he planned for us long ago." **I am a workmanship of God.**

CHAPTER 9

Immorality Nullifies Authentic Identity

Moral is a word of Latin origin, which comes from the term /*moris*/ which means: "custom". It is a set of beliefs, customs, values and norms of a person or a social group, which functions as a guide to act and live. That is, morality guides which actions are correct and which are incorrect.

¿Why does the power of spiritual identity depend on moral purity?

Morality is the sum of knowledge acquired about the highest and noblest things, which a person respects in his or her conduct. Beliefs about morality are generalized and codified in a certain culture or in a certain social group, so morality regulates the behavior of its members. On the other hand, morality is often identified with physical desires such as nuclear energy, which is unleashed with devastating destruction, or can be controlled and thus bring benefits. Scripture exhorts you to also flee from youthful passions.

2 Timothy 2:22 NTV
Run from anything that stimulates youthful lusts. Instead, pursue righteous living, faithfulness, love, and peace. Enjoy the companionship of those who call on the Lord with pure hearts.

It also exhorts you to guard your heart above all else.

Proverbs 4:23 NTV
Guard your heart above all else, for it determines the course of your life.

Something that is not done, that is why human beings are always involved in their own conflicts.

Galatians 5:16-17 NKJV
I say then: Walk in the Spirit, and you shall not fulfill the lust of the flesh. For the flesh lusts against the Spirit, and the Spirit against the flesh; and these are contrary to one another, so that you do not do the things that you wish."

What Does It Mean To Have Moral Freedom?

Moral freedom is having your physical impulses under the control of the Holy Spirit.

John 7:38 RVR1960
He who believes in Me, as the Scripture has said, out of his heart will flow rivers of living water.

Moral freedom is not the right to do what one wants; it is to do what must be done.

Is "*...to be strengthened with might through His*

Spirit in the inner man, that Christ may dwell in your hearts through faith; that you, being rooted and grounded in love, may be able to comprehend with all the saints ... to know the love of Christ which passes knowledge. Ephesians 3:16-19

God designed you with three internal drives. These are listed in order in the following Bible passage:

1 Thessalonians 5:23 NKJV
"Now may the God of peace Himself sanctify you completely; and may your whole spirit, soul, and body be preserved blameless at the coming of our Lord Jesus Christ".

It is difficult to separate the human spirit from the soul, however, the Word of God can do it.

Hebrews 4:12 NKJV
"For the Word of God is living and powerful, and sharper than any two-edged sword, piercing even to the division of soul and spirit..."

When you become a Christian, the Spirit of God was united with your human spirit. So that God dwells within you.

What Happens in Your Spirit?

Faith is not a blind leap into the dark; It is

discerning what God desires to accomplish in and through your life.

Your spirit is the home of FAITH.

The first function of faith is to believe in Christ for the salvation of the soul. The Holy Spirit then takes up residence in your spirit and confirms that you are a Christian.

Romans 8:16 NKJV
"The Spirit Himself bears witness with our spirit that we are children of God".

By faith alone, you are able to perceive and accept God's moral standards.

Your spirit will bring conviction to your mind when you are about to do something that is morally impure. On the other hand, in your spirit, your senses are "...exercised to discern good and evil" Hebrews 5:14.

The impulses of the flesh together with disobedience are sin, and that will sadden the Holy Spirit, causing his presence to be extinguished in you.

The wisdom of God dwells in your spirit.

Wisdom is seeing life from God's perspective. As you fill your soul with the Word of God, your spirit will experience wisdom.

Psalms 51:6 NKJV
"Behold, You desire truth in the inward parts, and in the hidden part You will make me to know wisdom."

A wise person is able to identify immorality as folly. On the other hand, the simple man is easily led into immorality.

Creativity is the ability to see a need, a task, or an idea from a new perspective.

This skill is especially important to be able to find a way out of temptation:

1 Corinthians 10:13 NJKV
"No temptation has overtaken you except such as is common to a man; but God is faithful, who will not allow you to be tempted beyond what you are able, but with the temptation will also make the way of escape, that you may be able to bear it."

Your Spirit is the Home of Communion

Communion is a function of your spirit with the Holy Spirit, while friendship is a function of our soul. You can have communion with other Christians, because your spirit is capable of communicating with their spirit.

1 John 1:7 NKJV
"...But if we walk in the light as He is in the light, we have fellowship one another..."

You can also have fellowship with the Lord because his Spirit dwells in you.

1 Corinthians 2:11 NKJV
"For what man knows the things of a man except the spirit of a man which is in him? Even so no one knows the things of God except the Spirit of God."

Moral purity is essential for communion, because the Spirit of God cannot have communion with sin.

2 Corinthians 6:14 NLT
Don't team up with those who are unbelievers. How can righteousness be a partner with wickedness? How can light live with darkness?

Your Spirit is the Abode of Worship

True worship is a function of the spirit. "God is Spirit; and those who worship him must worship him in spirit and truth" (John 4:24). Worship is destroyed when the truth of godly moral standards is rejected, thereby grieving the Holy Spirit.

The Importance of Discernment

The discernment of truth comes through the manifestation of that gift manifested in your spirit by the Holy Spirit.

1 Corinthians 2:10 NKJV
"...But God has revealed them to us through His Spirit; For the Spirit searches all things, yes, the deep things of God."

Besides:

1 Corinthians 2:14 RVR1960
"...But the natural man does not receive the things of the Spirit of God, for they are foolishness to him; nor can he know them, because they are spiritually discerned."

The discernment of wisdom will free you from the evil man and the strange woman.

Proverbs 2:12, 16 NKJV
12 To deliver you from the way of evil, From the man who speaks perverse things 16 To deliver you from the immoral woman, from the seductress who flatters with her words,

What is Happening in Your Soul?

The Greek word for "soul," /psuqué/, is pronounced

"pseuqué" and is the word from which the word psychology is derived. The soul is the executive part of our being. It receives information from our physical senses, and develops thoughts, feelings, and decisions based on the information.

When your soul makes decisions based on the guidance of the Holy Spirit, you will be engaged in the movement of the Spirit. On the contrary, if your soul makes decisions based solely on the impulses of the flesh, you will have a carnal mind. This will produce moral slavery, and death.

Romans 8:6-8 NKJV
6 "For to be carnally minded is death, but to be spiritually minded is life and peace. 7 Because the carnal mind is enmity against God; for it is not subject to the law of God, nor indeed can be; 8 So then, those who are in the flesh cannot pleased God".

To have the power of God and be powerfully used by Him, you must come to the point of submitting your mind, will, and emotions to the control of the Holy Spirit.

What's Happening in Your Body?

Just as your spirit opens your life to the spiritual world, your physical senses of taste, touch, sight, hearing, and smell open your life to the physical world. God created the physical senses, and as long as they are under the control of the Holy Spirit, they will bring joy and satisfaction to you, and those around you.

Powerful in Spirit

The goal of the Christian life is to produce love, which springs from a pure heart, a good conscience, and genuine faith.

1 Timothy 1:5 NLT
The purpose of my instruction is that all believers would be filled with love that comes from a pure heart, a clear conscience, and genuine faith."

This kind of love is only possible when you are experiencing moral freedom in your life. The essence of genuine love is to give, while the essence and goal of lust is to obtain. Love can always wait to give, but lust can never wait to get.

Genuine love consists of giving for other people's basic needs, without the motivation of personal gain.

CHAPTER 10

How to Be Free from Sinful Habits

The Word of God teaches you how-to live-in victory over the works of sin that fight within each one. The power of the Word of God gives you the tools to overcome temptation and be free from contamination, ties and oppressions, which are the causes of not defeating sin. What conquest brings to moral impurity, both in thoughts and body, is emphasized in Romans chapters 6 and 7. There the two ways that a Christian can live are taught.

James 1:21 NKJV
Receive with meekness the implanted word, which is able to save your souls.

If you meditate on the teachings of Romans 6-8, these passages will become the expression of your words, will, and emotions, rooted in God's truth. That will give you fruit that will build your spiritual life. The fruit of Romans 6 is victory over sin "...Sin shall not have dominion over you..."

Romans 6:14 NLT
Sin is no longer your master, for you no longer live under the requirements of the law. Instead, you live under the freedom of God's grace.

The True Identity

The fruit of Romans 8 is walking in the Spirit:

Romans 8:4 NKJV
That the righteous requirement of the law might be fulfilled in us who do not walk according to the flesh but according to the Spirit.

The other key to walking in moral freedom is knowing that you have already died to the sinful life that plagued you.

Do not provide for sinful habits. In Psalm 119:9-11 he gives the key to staying pure from youth.

"How can a young man cleanse his way? By keeping your word. The secret then is to keep the word. The word keep in its Hebrew root is /shama/ which means: Keep, pay attention, conserve, treasure, preserve.

The Word is not a book to simply read, it is to treasure it in the heart and follow the instructions by walking and living in them, it is the mirror in which we look at ourselves to see if we are aligned with the face of the Lord. A young man was continually tormented with imaginations, lasciviousness and covetous thoughts. He memorized Romans 6 and meditated on it, but he could not free himself from this bondage in his life. The reason was obvious: He had pornographic magazines stored in his room. In moments of temptation, he would take them out to see them.

The consequences of reading sensual material:
- You experience guilt by violating the moral laws that God wrote on his tablets. (10 commandments, you shall not covet) by looking at other women you are coveting what does not belong to you.
- You damage your marriage by committing mental adultery. (Jesus warned that just by looking at a woman you can commit adultery)
- You promote prostitution by paying for lewd materials.
- You open doors for mental illness, by having sensual pleasure without responsibility. You saturate your soul and mind with dirt, managing to sadden and quench the Holy Spirit.

Guard your heart and your eyes, which are the windows of the soul.

If you establish the practice of tolerating evil in order to enjoy a little of what you think is pleasurable, you lower your resistance to evil. Others are weakened by having constant access to reading false philosophies and concepts beneath the roots of this world. If you expose yourself to people who are tolerant of sin, sharing hours in their homes, this will lead to your conscience being cauterized, while you gradually lose your pure love for the Lord.

Compare the law of sin with the law of gravity.

It is probably difficult for you to grasp the fact that by faith "you are dead to sin." The Apostle Paul describes clearly in Romans 7:21-24, about the "law of sin." The law of sin continually operates in our members, which comes from unredeemed sinful flesh. However, when we walk in the Spirit seeking God, listening to praise and taking time to seek Him in prayer, we are nullifying and crucifying the desires of the flesh. Stop to analyze this example. The only thing the eagle has to do to stop its fall is to spread its wings, and the force of ascension will overcome the law of gravity.

Romans 8:2 NKJV
For the law of the Spirit of life in Christ Jesus has made me free from the law of sin and death.

Everything centers on Christ, because he gave us life in the midst of death, so that the works of the flesh would die in all those who enter into "the law of the Spirit of life."

Hold yourself accountable for victory, before the authorities established by God himself.

This is one of the most important steps to conquer habits. Many have testified that even after knowing the gospel, they have not been able to conquer their bad habit. It was only when they discreetly informed a parent, pastor, or other God-given authority about their moral defeat. By confessing and being free comes complete victory.

Every member of your body mus become an instrument of justice.

Both being dead to sin and being alive to God are essential to victory over habits. Paul combines these ideas in Romans 12:21 when he says, "Do not be overcome by evil, but overcome evil with good."

Learn to be sensitive to spiritual impulses.

God wants to manifest his true will through your life. You will only achieve this if you are living according to the law of the Spirit, and not according to the law of sin. Become a powerful instrument in the hands of God and never lose the identity that as a child of Him enables you to walk in the spirit and not in the flesh, understanding in the depths of your being what the sacred scriptures show you. :

Romans 8:1,5-6.NKJV

¹ There is therefore now no condemnation to those who are in Christ Jesus, who do not walk according to the flesh, but according to the Spirit... ⁵ For those who live according to the flesh set their minds on the things of the flesh; but those who live according to the Spirit, the things of the Spirit. ⁶ For to be carnally minded is death, but to be spiritually minded is life and peace.

CHAPTER 11

Repentance as a Security Code

Today you can visit church after church, from majestic cathedrals to small congregations, and rarely will you hear a preaching about repentance. The same thing happens in many evangelical churches throughout America and the entire world. Of course, there are churches that do not commit to this important biblical doctrine. A large number of so-called Christians have determined that repentance is a very offensive message to be preached, as well as the word "sin", "cross", condemnation and endless expressions from the Bible. In fact, entire denominations have removed these expressions, downplaying their importance.

In some congregations you will only hear instructions about how to be a successful businessman, how to be prosperous, but not a word that speaks of feeling the godly sadness for your sins.

These things are definitely biblical. But you will not hear a message of repentance like the one Peter preached on the day of Pentecost.

His preaching led many to freedom in Christ Jesus. Many modern preachers might be horrified at what Peter preached that day. Acts 2 shows us the context of the apostle's powerful message:

Acts 2:37 NKJV
Now when they heard this, they were cut to the heart, and said to Peter and the rest of the apostles, "Men and brethren, what shall we do?

As this verse demonstrates, there must be foreknowledge of sins before true repentance.

That is the purpose of the law: to make people aware of sins. The hearts of those people in Jerusalem were moved when they heard the Word of God and only then did, they recognize their sins. Peter responded to his desperate cry by instructing them this way:

Acts 2:38 NKJV
... "Repent, and let every one of you be baptized in the name of Jesus Christ for the remission of sins; and you shall receive the gift of the Holy Spirit."

What Does Repentance Mean?

True repentance produces pain and regret for the sins committed by failing God.

Repentence consists of experiencing such contrition that it leads to changing the course of actions.

Something simpler: contrition of the heart is turning from the action you were taking and going in the opposite direction. Repentance aligns you with the Lord again, returning the communion that the evil action had taken from you.

Repentance is the only way to obtain true joy and be restored. Sometimes they are small actions that are committed daily, in which you have to feel remorse and repent, asking God for forgiveness. There is no other way to enter the peace and rest of Christ but through the doors of repentance. Paul wrote to the Corinthians about the fruits of repentance:

2 Corinthians 7:10-11 NLT

10 For the kind of sorrow God wants us to experience lead us away from sin and results in salvation. There is no regret for that kind of sorrow. But worldly sorrow, which lacks repentance, results in spiritual death. 11 Just see what this godly sorrow produced in you! Such earnestness, such concern to clear yourselves, such indignation, such alarm, such longing to see me, such zeal, and such a readiness to punis wrong. You showed that you have done everything necessary to make things right.

It is important to know the letter that Paul wrote to the Corinthians. He exposed the sin of incest in the congregation, since no one had taken action on the matter. And because they overlooked this terrible sin, there was no sadness in their midst. So, Paul wrote a tough message to the church. So, when the people sat down to read the letter aloud, their hearts were moved. They repented, full of sadness and pain, and faced the shameful sin that was among them. Now Paul encouraged them, saying:

"See what the sadness of God did in you. It produced prudence, it brought an indignation against their own sin." Repentance is the only means by which those who are held captive by sin can be freed and restored.

Repentance and faith in the redeeming blood of Christ results in the remission of sins, which means forgiveness and freedom from the power of sin. According to Peter, there can be no conversion, freedom, or new birth without repentance.

Acts 3:19 NKJV
Repent therefore and be converted, that your sins may be blotted out; so that times of refreshing may come from the presence of the Lord.

In this same way, Paul preached to the Athenians:

Acts 17:30 NKJV
Truly, these times of ignorance God overlooked, but now commands all men everywhere to repent.

Jesus said that he had come for this very purpose:

Luke 5:32 NKJV
I have not come to call the righteous, but sinners to repentance.

Mark 2:17 NLT
When Jesus heard this, he told them: «Healthy people don't need a doctor, -- sick people do. I have come to call not those who think they are righteous, but those who know they are sinners».

Jesus compares himself to a doctor who goes where he is needed most. It is so absurd to think that Jesus would refuse to care for the needy, it is impossible just as a doctor cannot refuse to care for the sick. Perhaps Luke is even clearer when he writes:

Luke 24:46-47 NKJV
46 Then He said to them, "Thus it is written, and thus it was necessary for the Christ to suffer and to rise from the dead the third day, 47 and that repentance and remission of sins should be preached in His name to all nations, beginning at Jerusalem"

It is important to understand that captives cannot be won as long as they are comfortable in their crimes and sins. To make them understand the mercy of Jesus Christ they have to understand that his sins separate him from God, so they would be convicted and ready to completely abandon evil. This is the only way to wage war in the spiritual field. And this only comes from the Holy Spirit who convicts of sin.

No one can truly call Jesus Lord if their life has not been changed, and this requires a change of mind and heart.

No one can claim to love Jesus if their life does not show the fruits of their repentance. After confronting sin with the preaching of repentance, indescribable joy will begin to manifest in life. It is necessary to continue preaching and teaching the same message that the first church preached in Jerusalem on the day of Pentecost: repentance for the forgiveness of sins.

Today the gospel of convenience and supply is confusing millions.

Important question to ponder: what is the reason why many never preach repentance? Will they be afraid of losing people from their congregations? I am sure that God regrets churches that do not preach the message of repentance. In fact, I am convinced that the Holy Spirit departs in sadness from such churches.

With all this, I believe that there is something that grieves the heart of God even more than the fact of being negligent in preaching repentance.

And it is for those who confess their sins to continue living in unbelief. I speak of those who have had a true conviction of sin, but do not yet have the peace and joy that comes with the forgiveness that repentance brings.

Repentance leads to forgiveness and forgiveness should lead to joy and peace.

These people, however, have no such rest. On the contrary, they live in constant fear and insecurity of salvation. They continue to pray for their salvation and even try to get baptized again and again. They have simply never fully understood the power of forgiveness. Just as Isaiah said: "Poor thing, weary with the storm, without comfort..." Isaiah 54:11.

The oppression of sins, memories and reminders of past sins, must not be carried beyond the cross.

Any sadness for past sins, voluntarily imposed, must be cast into the streams of the blood of Christ. Finally, the time comes when everyone who follows Christ hears the words:

Matthew 11:28 NKJV
"Come to Me, all you who labor and are heavy laden, and I will give you rest."

The Lord calls all those who have repented and believed in his name, but who still cannot rejoice in it because they carry a heavy burden of guilt and condemnation. To all of these, God invites them to come to Him and hand over their heavy burden to Him, to be filled with joy in their hearts. When we do this, the Holy Spirit comes to take up residence in us.

Jesus called the Spirit "The Helper", whose name means "one who comes to be at your side." From then on, you will never again walk alone or in your own strength, but with the help of the Holy Spirit.

God gives you an additional promise when he says that he makes you... "make you complete in every good work to do His will, working in you what is well pleasing in his sight. through Jesus Christ, to whom be glory forever and ever. Amen" Hebrews 13:21.

Your destiny, your hope, your true identity as a chosen son is affirmed in the Heavenly Father to become a participant in the glory to come.

Now you know that you are forever free from the curse of loneliness and lack of security. Remember this:

1. Recognize that Jesus loves you and extends his grace and mercy to you.
2. Repent, asking God to bring upon you sadness and contrition for your sins.
3. Receive God's love and rest in his promise

to forgive you.
4. Trust the New Covenant that tells you: "I will be merciful to you and forgive all your sins. And I will form in you those things that are pleasing to my will."

You are not alone in this fight. He has sent his Holy Spirit, and the power of the Name of Jesus so that you can defeat the enemy, freeing yourself from all slavery. He is the immutable one, the force that will guide you and strengthen you in all your spiritual battles.

Pray with me: "Heavenly Father, thank you for sending Jesus Christ to be the way to reach you. I want you to always give me your approval as a Father and help me maintain my trust and faith in my future, which you have already given me. Deliver me from all self-deceptions so that I may always be free from all hypocrisy, be a son who honors and adores you in Spirit and truth. Thank you for that security that the Holy Spirit provides me to grow in grace and in your favor with a pleasant, patient and loving character. In the name of Jesus, amen".

CHAPTER 12

Maintaining Moral Purity

God has given you normal physical appetites; However, you were also born carrying the sinful nature in your genes. That at any moment they can awaken opposing the Holy Spirit, who dwells within each believer. Once a person lets evil actions take over, physical appetites will take control of spiritual desires. The process of incorrectly arousing sexual desires inappropriately is called falling under the dominion of the spirit of lasciviousness.

2 Corinthians 12:21 NLT
Yes, I am afraid that when I come again, God will humble me in your presence. And I will be grieved because many of you have not given up your old sins, You have not repented of your impurity, sexual immorality, and eagerness for lustful pleasure.

Galatians 5:19 NLT
When you follow the desires of your sinful nature, the results are very clear: sexual immorality, impurity, lustful pleasures...

Romans 7:8 NLT
But sin used this command to arouse all kinds of covetous desires within me! If there were no law, sin would not have the power.

1 Thessalonians 4:5 NKJV
Not in passion of lust, like the Gentiles who do not know God;

Concupiscence is the condition of the soul in which sensual lust is stronger than spiritual desires. When limitations on God-given desires are violated, there are immediately feelings of guilt. Very often the person at fault will attempt to return to a balance of impulses, only to discover that this is not possible.

Sexual passions do not automatically return to lower levels of intensity. Solomon explained this problem when he wrote about the consequences when a young man loses his purity in the house of a harlot.

Proverbs 2:18-19 NKJV
[18] For her house leads down to death, and her paths to the dead; [19] none who go to her return, nor do they regain the paths of life."

The consequences are explained more fully in the following biblical passage:

Proverbs 5:20-23 NKJV
[20] For why should you, my son, be enraptured by an immoral woman, and be embraced in the arms of a seductress? [21] For the ways of man are before the eyes of the Lord, and He ponders all his paths. [22] His own iniquities entrap the wicked man, and

he is caught in the cords of his sin. ²³ He shall die for lack of instruction, and in the greatness of his folly he shall go astray.

Another problem is found in the area of concupiscence and that is that sensual desires continue to grow as sin is exercised. Moral impurity is like a muddy pit, the more a man struggles within it the deeper he sinks into it. A reprobated person is one who has rejected the truth, who has seared his conscience, and who believes his own lie. The lie is that sensual pleasure is the maximum in his life.

Romans 1:25-28 NKJV
²⁵ "who exchanged the truth of God for the lie, and worshiped and served the creature rather than the Creator, who is blessed forever. Amen. ²⁶ For this reason God gave them up to vile passions. For even their women exchanged the natural use for what is against nature. ²⁷ Likewise also the men… ²⁸ And even as they did not like to retain God in their knowledge, God gave them over to a debased mind…."

The Dilemma of Being Double Minded Completely Disrupts Correct Identity

When conscience is violated through an act of moral impurity, sensual impulses increase. At that moment the mind, will and emotions find themselves in the middle of two opposing forces. On the one hand, the soul of the believer wants to be spiritual, on the other hand the soul likes to be sensual. This "double soul" condition is precisely what James describes in his epistle. Explaining that there is an inconstancy in the actions of said person. The term man is meaningless, because it gives no idea of either the cause or the remedy. Therefore, he tries to compensate for what is missing in his spiritual life with religious effort, the result of which is a pseudo-religious façade.

On the outside he appears to have a strong spiritual character, but under pressure, he manifests a carnal nature.

Soon another state develops in the soul, pseudo-intellectualism. With weak spiritual desires and strong sensual impulses, he begins to discuss and debate philosophical ideas that he hears from others, or that he invents on his own. Paul warns about these pseudo-intellectuals:

Titus 3:10-11 NLT
10 If people are causing divisions among you, give a first and second warning. After that, have nothing more to do with them. 11 For people like that have turned away from the truth, and their own sins condemn them.

He explains that they argue because they have moral deviations, and they know it.

Why Would Two Christians Differ About the Same Activity?

The more a person progresses toward concupiscence, and subsequently to reprobation, the less he is bothered by the things that previously troubled his conscience.

First of all, the Holy Spirit is saddened, and therefore the signal he sends to rebuke the conscience is extinguished. Second, the Word of God is rejected in the mind, while it is replaced by human reasoning. There is no sin that cannot be rationalized by speculation.

Finally, lust tends to increase, and from a passion it passes to an even lower immorality. God describes the full range of immorality in Romans 1. Three times in this chapter we find the phrase, "God handed them over..." It is important to note that in Scripture this phrase is not followed by a period, but by the word "a.". God does not reject the person; rather he hands him over to the consequences of his own choice.

Lasciviousness Becomes Perversion

In Romans 1, the first mention of God "handing over" a person is found in verse 24. God first explains that they had the testimony of his nature and deity, by his creation (verses 19-20), but They refused to glorify him and recognize him as God, and they became vain in their reasoning.

Romans 1:19-20 NLT
19 They know the truth about God because He has made it obvious to them. 20 For ever since the world was created, people have seen the earth and sky. Through everything God made, they can clearly see his invisible qualities – his eternal power and divine nature. So they have no excuse for not knowing God.

After their foolish hearts were darkened, they exchanged the glory of the Holy God for a corruptible god who would allow them to do the things they wanted to do.

Romans 1:24 NKJV
Therefore God also gave them up to uncleanness, in the lusts of their heart, to dishonor their bodies among themselves.

The filth of lasciviousness will include the first level of sensuality, identified in Scripture as concupiscence. At this first level, God gives the person to be the object of his own sensual desires. If this person does not repent, then he will continue in his conscience to replace the lie with the truth.

Romans 1:26 ^{NKJV}
For this reason God gave them up to vile passions.

The wages of lasciviousness is more lasciviousness, and the wages of sensuality is destruction through shameful passions.

The person is not born with lust, but rather voluntarily chooses to participate in sensuality. Many today fall victims to rapists, who at an early age destabilize their identity, which produces that duality in their minds. The Church has the power of God through the Name of Jesus to remove the mark of abuse as long as the person wishes to do so. Her first step will be to forgive the abuser and recognize that the Blood of Christ frees him by forgiving all of his sins.

Natural Curiosity

There is nothing wrong with natural curiosity, as long as it is under the control of the Holy Spirit. Eve could satisfy her curiosity by eating the fruit of all the trees in the garden, except one. The limitation that God imposed on Eve is identical to the limitation that is imposed when it comes to curiosity.

Do not try to acquire knowledge of evil through experience because that will tarnish and weaken your true identity.

Your conscience is a God-given alarm system. It activates every time you approach evil, or evil approaches you. Your conscience will tell you when something is wrong, even when your friends or teachers try to convince you that it is right. The first sign that your consciousness has been awakened is that the question comes to mind, "Is it right for me to do this?" If you do not heed this sign, then you will begin to think of reasons to sanctify the activity in question.

Many Think that the Limits Established by God are Exaggerated.

The first question that Satan asked Eve exaggerated and ridiculed the limitation that God had placed on her: "...Why has God said to you: Do not eat of every tree of the garden?"

Genesis 3:1 NLT
The serpent was the shrewdest of all the wild animals the Lord God had made. One day he asked the woman, "Did God really say you must not eat the fruit from any of the trees in the garden? (the tree of the knowledge of good and evil).

Eve went beyond these words by adding, "...you will not even touch him..."

Genesis 3:3 NLT

It's only the fruit from the tree in the middle of the garden that we are not allowed to eat. God said, "You must not eat it or even touch it; if you do, you will die".

By going beyond the Word of God, he made himself vulnerable to Satan. If he cannot get you to deny the Word of God, he will tempt you to distort its meaning, or add restrictions to it that were not in God's intentions.

Sensual Approach

Hearing Satan's mockery, and then his denial of the Word of God, doubts were planted in Eve's mind regarding what God had really said, and his reasons for saying it. She continued contemplating the forbidden fruit and began to covet it.

James 1:14-15 NKJV

14 But each one is tempted when he is drawn away by his own desire and enticed. 15 Then, when desire has conceived, it gives birth to sin; and sin, when it is full-grown, brings forth death.

Violation of Consciousness

Eve reached out her hand, took the fruit, and ate it, in direct violation of God's Word.

If you find yourself enslaved by some sensual habit, you can probably remember the time you consciously did what you knew in your heart was wrong. Perhaps you were expecting, like Eve, God's immediate judgment, not recognizing that spiritual death had already occurred, along with invisible bondage.

Romans 6:16 NKJV
"Do you not know that to whom you present yourselves slaves to obey, you are that one's slaves whom you obey, whether of sin leading to death, or of obedience leading to righteousness?"

Every time you ignore a warning from your conscience, you are violating established boundaries. God calls that a sin.

Genesis 3:7-8 NLT
⁷ At that moment their eyes were opened, and they suddenly felt shame at their nakedness. So they sewed fig leaves together to cover themselves. ⁸ When the cool evening breezes were blowing, the man and his wife heard the Lord God walking about in the garden. So they hid from the Lord God among the trees.

Guilt is to the conscience what pain is to the nervous system. The function of pain is to warn you that some damage is occurring, and that if you don't make some change, you will suffer further damage. Similarly, guilt was designed by God to warn you that you are harming yourself, and that your only recourse is to turn from your sin and come to God in repentance. Sin causes shame and fear.

Genesis. 3:10 NLT

10 He replied, —"I heard you walking in the garden, so I hid. I was afraid because I was naked."

Adam and Eve responded to their transgression by joining fig leaves to cover their nakedness from one another, and then to hide from God.

These responses violated the very purpose of guilt, which is to bring repentance, and restore fellowship with Him.

Incomplete repentance leads to religious compensation (fig leaf style) in order to be respectable to those around you.

CHAPTER 13

True Identity and Eternal Destiny

Having life as a human being with indescribable mysteries and having an eternal destiny of glory or inexpressible horror is a weight that can overwhelm you with fear or fill you with glory with joy and jubilation, which cannot be described. Whether one or the other occurs depends largely on whether or not you know the answers to the concerns where you are headed.

1 Peter 2:9 NKJV

But you are a chosen generation, royal priesthood, a holy nation, His own special people, that you may proclaim the praises of Him who called you out of darkness into His marvelous light.

1 Peter 2:9 NLT

But you are not like that, for you are a chosen people. You are royal priests, a holy nation, God's very own possession. As a result, you can show others the goodness of God, for he called you out of the darkness into his wonderful light.

- Who are you?
- How did you obtain your identity?
- What are you here for?

Rarely will you find such clear answers to these

three questions as in the text you just read, in which you will find the obvious answers of the Word of God for you.

Who are you?

It is evident that the Apostle Peter is addressing Christians with a defined identity in Christ, if this is the reason for who they are through Him and for Him. This is why they are here as Christians.

In the aforementioned biblical text, five ways of describing identity are presented, thus answering the question of who we are.

1.- But you are a chosen race.
You must understand that the identity mentioned here is group, which refers to the church. Even so, it also alludes to the individual, because it does not refer to a racial lineage, the chosen lineage is neither black, nor white, nor red or yellow-skinned, nor any other race in particular. The chosen lineage is about new people from all peoples, races, colors and cultures who for now are foreigners and pilgrims in the world.

Verse 11, **"Beloved, I appeal to you as strangers and pilgrims..."**

What gives us identity is neither color nor culture but the fact of being chosen, Christians are not a defined race; If they are not the chosen race, we have been chosen from every race, regardless of which group we belong to. This is why it is so amazing and of particular importance to each of us; Yes, a "chosen lineage" because it is made up of men and women who were chosen from all races.

So the first identity we have is that of being chosen. God chose us, it was not because of race or any other condition, only He has been pleased to choose us. Who are you? a chosen one, it is still difficult for you to understand why it was like that. There was nothing about you or me that made us of more value than any other human being. It is not because we earned it or deserved it, in fact it is not because we meet certain conditions or requirements to achieve it, it was more established before we were born. This is one more of the mysteries of the greatness and wonders of the sovereignty of the one true God, this should impact us intensely, so the only thing that remains for us is to fall at his feet kneeling in gratitude for his immense love without conditions. , understanding it should lead us to fidelity and obedience to the purposes established for each of those that have been chosen.

2.- We are an acquired people.
The word acquired has to do with the Greek word /peripoiesis/ which means, preservation, possession and attaining.

When God chose us, he saw us trapped in sin because of us and condemned and he had mercy on us. Not only were we chosen; We were also acquired by Him from him. We are not only the object of His choice, but also of His mercy, to be His possession, that is, we belong to Him. Even this is affirmed by the Word of God:

Psalms 33:12 NLT
What joy for the nation whose God is the Lord, whose people he has chosen as his inheritance.

1 Peter 2:10 NLT
«Once you had on identity as a people; now you are God's people. Once you received no mercy, now you have received God's mercy."

I am chosen and He acquired me by paying a great price on the cross, He gave me the grace of His love, we are loved by the limitless manifestation of His love. God did not choose us to stay apart, He has done it to surround us with the great mercy of He approached us to help us, forgive us and save us. We receive the identity we have not based on our actions, but because someone has acted on us with mercy.

3.- We belong to God.
This is expressed twice. Verse 9: "You are a peculiar people for God's possession." Verse 10 "You once were not a people, but now you are the people of God." They are chosen by God; to whom

God manifested grace and favor; and the result of all this is that God has taken us as his own belonging.

Now, we know that absolutely everything belongs to God. So in a sense we are all part of God's possessions. So this has to refer to something special and of course, it is, we are God's inheritance, those with whom he will spend eternity.

2 Corinthians 6:16 NLT
And what union can there be between God's temple and idols? For we are the temple of the living God. As God said:
«I will live in them
And walk among them.
I will be their God,
And they will be my people.

4.- We are called to be saints.
"You are a holy nation."
Chosen by God and now we belong to him and have received mercy from him; and for this reason we are no longer part, nor do we belong to the system of this world.

We were set apart, we existed for Him, invested and surrounded by His holiness, consequently just as He is Holy so are we. We share his character, because he chose us, out of pity he acquired us, if you are not able to behave and conduct yourself in this new life in a holy way, you will act outside of his character and designs. Acting like this contradicts your nature as a Christian and denies your new identity which is holiness before the Lord, if you and I are called to be saints, to finally be:

5. Royal Priesthood.
We were chosen by God and He reached us and now we belong to Him and we are saints like Himself and royal priests before God. The first point that stands out is that we have immediate and direct access to God, it is not necessary to have another human priest as an intermediary. God himself has provided an Intermediary, that is, a mediator between God and man; Jesus Christ. And second, we play a high and active role in the presence of God. We were not chosen, pitied, possessed, and sanctified just to pass time doing nothing. We have been called to minister in the presence of God. Now every aspect of our lives must be dedicated to the priestly task. We are not called to be outside the presence of God but inside it. You should never find yourself in a neutral, passive or indifferent zone, the life you now lead is either a life of service in spiritual worship (Romans 12:1-2), or a life out of character.

Romans 12:1-2 NLT
¹ And so, dear brothers and sisters, I plead with you to give your bodies to God because of all he has done for you. Let them be a living and holy

sacrifice, the kind he will find acceptable. This is truly the way to worship him. ² Don't copy the behavior and customs of this world, but let God transform you into a new person by changing the way you think. Then you will learn to know God's will for you, which is good and pleasing and perfect.

So you can see that the identity question of "Who am I?"—involves asking the second question, "What am I here for?"

Your true identity in Christ leads you to your true destiny. Remember that you and I have been chosen, pitied, possessed, and holy. All with one purpose: to serve as priests. And Peter clearly describes the heart of that ministry.

How Have We Received This Identity?

But before we answer the question of what we are here for, let's pause and answer the middle question: How did we get this identity?

The answer is evidently obvious, we receive our identity from God himself, in fact identity is our relationship with Him, this is what Peter declares all this in a summary at the end of verse 9. He refers to God in this way:

"He who called them out of darkness into his marvelous light." The light in which we live is the light of being chosen, pitied, belonging, sanctified and priestly, becoming so because God called us, changing every spectrum of darkness into shining light.

What I want to imply is that the experience of walking in the light, of being chosen, experiencing that identity is the effect of the sovereign call of God, affirming in a sure way that He Himself gave us the identity that we have and possess.

Remember that therefore identity leads you to your eternal destiny, you are therefore chosen, pitied, acquired, holy; and all with the purpose of being a royal priesthood. It is evident that Peter was even more specific when he communicates to us the precise reason for our existence. In verse 9 he tells us the reason is this:

"so that you may proclaim the praises of him who called you out of darkness into his marvelous light."

This is the destiny of a royal priest, to make known the glories of the king. Today the concept of one's own identity is constantly mentioned. How do you see yourself? is an important question, it is important that you fully understand that the specific approach from a biblical perspective to this question is that genuine Christian identity is not defined in terms of who you are as an individual, but in terms of what God does and the relationship May He believe in you and the destiny He has prepared for you, in short as a Christian, you cannot talk about your identity without talking about God's action on your own life, His relationship with you and the purpose that was established for you. Therefore it is evident that if you develop a true biblical understanding about the identity of a Christian you will come to the conclusion that it is radically centered on God and not on man.

Achieving identity is not the goal, but the means to the priestly function that Peter defines as the proclamation of the excellencies of him who called us out of darkness into his admirable light.

God made us what we are so that we can proclaim the excellence of his greatness by choosing us; the excellence of his grace in taking pity on us; the excellence of his authority and power to possess us; the excellence of his power and purity in making us holy.

In other words, he has given you and me the identity to proclaim his identity and it is in turn manifested through us. God made us what we are so that we can make him known. The purpose of our identity is to manifest his identity, the reason for our identity is so that the excellence of God may be manifested in us.

Therefore, being a Christian is equal to making

known the splendor and majesty of his glorious presence, it is time that you begin to manifest it in every area of your life on a daily basis, when your actions show the excellencies of God, people will listen with more enthusiasm, it is another way of saying that your identity is for God's purpose. God made us what we are to show the world what He is and to lead us to eternal life.

Bibliography

Rainbow Study Bible. Reina-Valera Version, Revision 1960, Biblical text copyright© 1960, Bible Society in Latin America, Nashville, Tennessee, ISBN: 1-55819-555-6.

Biblia Plenitud. Reina-Valera Version, 1960 Revision, ISBN: 089922279X, Editorial Caribe, Miami, Florida.

Strong James, LLD, S.T.D., *Strong's Comprehensive Concordance of the Bible,* Editorial Caribe, Inc., Thomas Nelson, Inc., Publishers, Nashville, Tennessee - Miami, FL, EE.UU., 2002. ISBN: 0- 89922-382-6.

Vine, W.E. *Expository Dictionary of the Words of the Old Testament and New Testament.* Editorial Caribe, Inc./División Thomas Nelson, Inc., Nashville, TN. ISBN: 0-89922-495-4, 1999.

Biblia Plenitud. 1960 Reina-Valera Revision, Copyright© 1994, Editorial Caribe, Miami, Florida. ISBN: 089922279X

Scofield Annotated Bible, 1960 Reina-Valera Revision. Copyright © 1987 Spanish Publications. (Scofield Bible)

Keyton, Dr. Bree M., Jezebel vs. Elijah, Copyright © 2001 Black Horse Press, San Diego, California. ISBN: 9781582750521

Vine, W.E. Expository Dictionary of the Words of the Old Testament and New Testament. Editorial Caribe, Inc. /División Thomas Nelson, Inc., Nashville, TN, ISBN: 0-89922-495-4,

1999. *(Vine's Expository Dictionary of Old and New Testament Words, Thomas-Nelson, Inc.)*

The Thompson Reference Bible, Reina- Valera 1960 Version copyright © 1987 The B.B. Kirkbride Bible Company, Inc. Y Editorial Vida, Miami, FL. ISBN: 0829714448 (original The Thompson Chain Reference © 1983 The B.B. Kirkbride Bible Company, Inc., Indianapolis, Indiana.)

Blue Letter Bible. Sowing circle. ‹http://blueletterbible.org›

Wikipedia. Wikimedia. ‹http://www.wikipedia.org›

New Living Translation Bible

www.ingramcontent.com/pod-product-compliance
Lightning Source LLC
Chambersburg PA
CBHW060529100426
42743CB00009B/1470